Bead Crochet Basics

22 JEWELRY PROJECTS

W9-BCL-599

Bead Crochet Basics

22 JEWELRY PROJECTS

Candice Sexton

KALMBACH BOOKS

Kalmbach Books
21027 Crossroads Circle
Waukesha, Wisconsin 53186
www.Kalmbach.com/Books

© 2014 Candice Sexton

All rights reserved. Except for brief excerpts for review, this book and DVD may not be reproduced in part or in whole by electronic means or otherwise without written permission of the publisher.

Lettered step-by-step photos and illustrations by the author. All other photography © 2014 Kalmbach Books except where otherwise noted.

The jewelry designs in *Bead Crochet Basics* are the copyrighted property of the author and contributors, and they may not be taught or sold without permission. Please use them for your education and personal enjoyment only.

Although efforts have been made to ensure the accuracy of the information presented, the publisher is not responsible for any losses or other damages that may result from the use of the information in this book.

Published in 2014

18 17 16 15 14   1 2 3 4 5

Manufactured in China

ISBN: 978-0-87116-446-9
EISBN: 978-1-62700-108-3

Editor: Mary Wohlgemuth
Art director: Lisa Bergman
Technical Editor: Julia Gerlach
Photographers: James Forbes, William Zuback
Pattern tester: Rifka Boswell

Publisher's Cataloging-in-Publication Data

Sexton, Candice, author.
    Bead crochet basics & beyond : 27 jewelry projects / Candice Sexton.

        pages : color illustrations ; cm + 1 DVD (sd., col. ; 4 ¾ in.)

    Accompanying DVD demonstrates how to begin a bead crochet rope.
    Issued also as an ebook.
    ISBN: 978-0-87116-446-9

    1. Beadwork–Patterns. 2. Beadwork–Handbooks, manuals, etc. 3. Crocheting–Handbooks, manuals, etc.
    4. Jewelry making–Handbooks, manuals, etc. I. Title. II. Title: Bead crochet basics and beyond

TT860 .S49 2014
739.27

Contents

Welcome to bead crochet!

I discovered seed beads and beadweaving in 2001. While traveling for work, I became frustrated with all the seed beads in little containers, so many tools, and large beading mats. Beading on airplanes often was a memorable experience (and not in a good way).

Enter bead crochet.

Like many bead enthusiasts, I love taking classes. I thoroughly soak in the atmosphere of like-minded people enjoying a shared interest, whether it's at a favorite bead shop, a friend's home, or at a big convention. So I took my first bead crochet class at a bead shop.

While thinking to myself after class, "I've got this! I can make a bead crochet bracelet at home," the truth was that I needed hands-on, detailed help to go from the first steps of bringing the bead down the thread to starting the bead crochet tube. As many of you can relate, eight hours later, I had a bunch of grapes (also known as misplaced beads), a sore back, and frazzled nerves.

I want to help you conquer that learning curve, and save you some aches and pains. *Bead Crochet Basics* is the result of intensive study on my part followed by more than 10 years of teaching across the country to many eager, including some frustrated, beginners. I have incorporated my background in engineering and construction into my teaching. I'm always deconstructing a technique, breaking it down into easily understood, graphic steps that make sense to me, making the technique almost failsafe.

This book-with-DVD includes ideas, shortcuts, techniques, and tools that make bead crochet easily portable, understandable, and relaxing.

All the beginner techniques I've learned and have taught to students are here. Getting past the first three rows (a constant phrase in my beginner classes) is the initial goal of *Bead Crochet Basics*. After that hurdle, I will help you progress and become enthralled with wonderful patterns that add exciting graphic designs to your work.

I wish you many happy, relaxing moments as you enjoy learning and mastering bead crochet.

– CANDICE SEXTON

ABOUT THIS BOOK AND DVD

Learning bead crochet is best achieved in logical, progressive steps. The projects open with the easiest, and they gradually increase in complexity as your skills grow. You'll find 10 numbered technique lessons interspersed throughout the projects, placed at just the right point in your learning curve. I don't repeat this common information in every project; simply refer back to the lessons as needed.

While some beginners may need to—or want to—do many beginner projects, if you've had a little successful experience with bead crochet, feel free to start beyond the first three projects.

Included with each project are thread types and sizes. In the beginner projects, you'll use thick thread, large seed beads such as 6° s or 8°s, and large crochet hooks. As you move along, you'll use smaller beads, such as 11° seed beads, and start to work with more complex patterns. The small seed beads require thinner threads and smaller crochet hooks. Typically, the latter projects also close using the important invisible join technique, which is explained in Technique 6 on p. 38.

The DVD at the back of this book is my "quick-start" lesson for beginners: It focuses solely on the steps necessary to start the slip-stitch method of bead crochet (the way all my bead crochet ropes begin). By showing you close-up, in action, and talking you through the start, I can help you avoid some of the pitfalls that beginners often encounter.

Basics

What is bead crochet?

Bead crochet is a crochet technique that incorporates beads into the finished piece. You can use beads of all types in bead crochet: seed beads, fire-polished beads, crystals, and unusually shaped beads such as daggers. Although you may encounter other techniques for bead crochet, such as the European or single-stitch method, all the projects in this book fall into the broad category of rope-style bead crochet. They all use the basic slip-stitch method of crocheting that's explained on p. 14 and on the accompanying DVD.

BEAD CROCHET TOOLKIT

The simple kit shown in the photo below is used for all the projects. It includes a bobbin, a Big Eye needle, a roundnose pin, a tapestry needle, a crochet hook, a locking stitch marker, and cord—all explained in detail on the next pages.

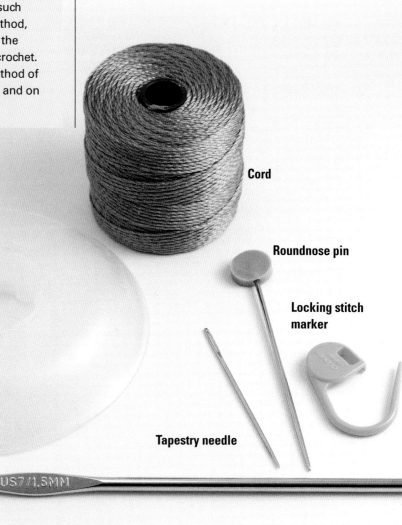

Cord

Roundnose pin

Locking stitch marker

Bobbin

Tapestry needle

Steel crochet hook

US7/1.5MM

Big Eye needle

In addition to the items shown, you'll need several familiar beadwork items:
- Bead trays or bead mats that keep seed beads in place
- Fine, sharp embroidery scissors
- Task lighting
- Magnifiers or reading glasses for close-up work
- Small pair of chainnose jewelry pliers to pull a long-eye needle through the bead hole
- Wire cutters to cut memory wire or other shaping wire
- Measuring tape
- Bead scoop or metal triangle to pick up seed beads
- Crimping pliers or a T-pin for breaking unwanted beads

As you move to more challenging projects, you'll need to add a few items (see p. 37).

Each project will call for additional materials needed. The lists include closures and finishing items such as focal beads, bead cones or caps, lobster claw or other clasps, jump rings for the clasp, and extra beads for fringe such as crystals, pearls, Czech beads, or sterling silver.

The Bead Crochet Toolkit contains the fundamental tools that you will use for almost every bead crochet project in this book. Some of the items you will recognize from beadwork or kumihimo. You may also recognize a few from yarn crocheting or knitting.

Medium or large bobbins
The first step in any bead crochet project is stringing beads onto cord. To avoid tangled beads and cord, use plastic bobbins made for kumihimo to wrap strung beads quickly and securely. They'll hold your work as you crochet and are great for safe and easy transport as well. They come in small, medium, and large sizes. Use one or two medium bobbins for bracelet projects and five or six medium or two large bobbins for necklaces.

Big Eye needle
The best method for stringing beads onto crochet cord is to use a Big Eye needle, which has an opening all along its length. These come in varying lengths, widths, and materials. For bead sizes from the largest down to 11º seed beads, Big Eye needles provide length to string on many beads at once, and they hold up well to frequent use. Smaller bead sizes such as 15ºs and some cylinder beads require thinner Big Eye needles (more details on those later).

If in doubt about what type of needle to buy, consider the size of the cord as well as bead size. Two thicknesses must pass through a bead when stringing due to the tail. Using a needle that's too large for your seed beads can break the needle and the beads.

Roundnose pin
A crochet pin, macramé pin, or tapestry needle works well for picking out knots in your work. Its rounded nose won't split the cord. You can also use the pin to help push out beads that sink into the rope. An awl may work too—just be sure it has a rounded, not sharp, tip.

Tapestry needle
A small tapestry needle is needed for finishing every project. Whether using a focal bead as your closure, using end cones and a hook, or closing with an invisible join, each closure is finished using a small tapestry needle.

Sharp scissors
Use sharp scissors to cut your cord. Dull scissors will fray your ends and slow down your work. Embroidery scissors are available in many sizes and work with all weights of cords used in bead crochet.

Locking stitch marker
What happens when you want to stop crocheting? Your rope can easily unravel if the cord is pulled in the slightest way. Use a locking stitch marker (commonly used in knitting and widely available) secured through your last loop to hold the work in place until you are ready to begin again.

Unlike safety pins, locking stitch markers will not split your cord. And they come in great colors! (Thanks to Linda Lehman, a contributor to this book, who taught me this hint—it is a winner.)

Crimping pliers or a T-pin
Occasionally you'll find a misplaced bead as you're checking your pattern after stringing. Use crimping pliers to crush the bead and then remove it. Or, better yet, insert a T-pin into the bead and angle the pin while applying pressure until the bead breaks.

Crochet hooks

The hooks used in bead crochet are made of steel and have very narrow tips ranging from about 1mm to 2.5mm. The sizing system varies among manufacturers, but each size has a number assigned to it. (Note that this sizing convention is completely different than the system used with aluminum or plastic hooks for yarn crochet.)

The style of crochet hook you choose affects the consistency of your piece and the durability of the crochet hook's tip.

A key feature is a wide shaft or a foam grip to ease wrist, hand, and finger strain. Pay attention to how your hands feel as you work—your hands will get tired, especially when first starting to bead crochet, so choose a comfortable hook. I slide a foam grip onto my hook to allow for a natural grip.

Many brands of hooks are sold with a wide cushioned thumb section. Additionally, if you are handy with polymer clay, you can mold and bake the clay onto a stainless steel crochet hook that fits your hand and grip comfortably. Finally, beautifully handcrafted handles made from fine wood are available at yarn shops and online.

> **TIP** If you notice the crochet hook's tip becoming sharp, buy a new hook. The sharpness will pierce and separate your cord, which weakens your piece.

Go to your favorite bead shop or yarn shop and try out different crochet hooks to determine which style works best for you. Whichever hook style or brand you choose, you will develop a preference as you become more experienced.

The size of your beads and the type and size/weight of your cord are the two primary factors in determining what size crochet hook to use. The larger the hook number, the smaller the hook tip and the thinner the cord used.

Susan Bates and Boye are common steel hook brands suggested for bead crochet. As bead crochet becomes more and more popular, you'll likely find other brands such as Clover, Tulip, and Addi readily available.

Beginner bead crocheters should use a large crochet hook such as a size 6 (1.6mm) or 7 (1.5mm) while learning to bead crochet. This is also generally good advice for all levels. If you are having trouble keeping the hook tip around the cord, go up a size in crochet hook to see if it makes a difference in your crocheting.

Cord and thread

Match the color of your cord to the predominant color of your beads if you want it to blend with the beadwork. Cord weight and flexibility determines how your piece will drape, if it will be stiff or supple, how easy the piece is to crochet, and of course, how the piece looks. A good rule to follow is: the smaller the bead, the thinner the cord you should use.

When choosing your cord, consider the following:
• How you want the piece to look when finished
• Do you want a supple drape or do you want a stiff piece?
• How much wear and tear the piece will get in its lifetime
• How you will finish the piece (focal bead, cone ends, or invisible join)
• Are you using crystals, daggers, or other sharp-edge beads (other than seed beads)

Cord choices range from fine to heavyweight (left to right in the photo on the right).

GUIDE

Seed bead size	Cord	Needle	Hook size
6º and 8º	C-Lon #18 nylon cord S-Lon #18 Silkon #3 cord Tuff Cord #3 or #5	Big Eye needle	6 (1.6mm) or 7 (1.5mm)
8º and 11º	C-Lon Tex 135 Tuff Cord #2 #20 cotton	Big Eye needle	8 (1.25–1.4mm)
11º	C-Lon Micro Cord Tuff Cord #2 #20, 30, or 40 cotton (#40 for Delica cylinders)	Big Eye needle; 9cm Bead Threaders thin long-eye needle by Kawaguchi	9 (1.15–1.25mm)
12º–15º	C-Lon Micro Cord Tuff Cord #0 or #1 #40 cotton	9cm Bead Threader (fine-gauge long-eye needle by Kawaguchi)	10–14 (1.15–.9mm)

Read on for guidelines for different situations, and use the chart above for quick reference.

Beginners are most successful using thick cord such as C-Lon Bead Cord or other heavyweight nylon. Thick cord gives you more cord to hold with your hook, provides support for the beads, and makes it easier to learn the technique.

Yarn used in traditional crochet (such as #3 size) shouldn't be used for bead crochet; the yarn will fuzz up due to friction from the beads sliding along its length.

Most nylon cords are good choices for all bead crochet projects. Fine nylon, such as fineweight C-Lon, does not stretch, is very good for small beads (11ºs and 15ºs), and comes in many colors.

For crocheting with 8º and 11º seed beads, high-quality #20 weight cotton used in traditional crochet and tatting works well. Look for brand names Flora, Lizbeth, Gutermann, Cebelia, Presencia, and Opera. Fineweight nylon is a good choice as well. Heavyweight cord won't work with 11º beads since it can't go through the bead hole easily.

Using very thin thread (#40, for example, or Gutermann topstitch thread) for 8º beads isn't recommended; it won't support the 8º bead hole.

For 15º beads or projects that use both 11ºs and 15ºs, use fineweight C-Lon Micro nylon cord or Lizbeth, Flora, Cebelia, or Elite in a #40 weight.

Perle cotton is widely available but tends to split and fuzz up easily; both problems lead to the thread breaking, so I don't recommend using perle cotton for bead crochet.

Stringing the beads

If you are making a project that uses one color of bead or an assorted mix of bead colors like the bracelets on p. 28, stringing order of beads won't matter: Just thread the Big Eye needle and string the specified number of beads.

However, many of the projects in this book use patterns made of bead colors and sometimes varying sizes or types of beads. For patterns like these, the order in which you string the beads is critical for creating the desired pattern. You must pick up beads in the order shown in the stringing pattern.

Slide the beads down the cord and do not cut the cord! Simply unroll the length you need from the spool as you string more beads.

The last bead you string is the first bead crocheted. Bead crochet patterns generally specify which place to start stringing your beads, whether it is at the beginning of the written bead pattern or at the end, with the last row. Most of the patterns in this book are strung following the stringing pattern from left to right and top to bottom.

STRING THE BEADS ON THE CORD

Place your beads in small piles in the order you will be stringing the beads (label the piles if it helps you). Open the Big Eye needle at the center and place the cord into the needle, pulling it down toward the bottom and leaving a comfortable length for the tail. Do not cut the cord; keep it on the spool **[A]**. As you add beads, wrap the beaded cord around the spool or a bobbin to keep them manageable.

String from left to right in a pattern unless otherwise specified. In the sample pattern below from the 5-around Hibiscus Flower Bracelet, which uses all 6° seed beads, you'll string a color A bead, a B, a C, a D, and an E, and repeat in the same order until you have strung all 62 rows.

As you string, slide beads down the cord until all the beads called for are strung. Remove the Big Eye needle carefully and slide the beads farther down the cord, leaving about 12" (30cm) of working cord. Remember, do not cut the cord.

STRINGING PATTERN

1A, 1B, 1C, 1D, 1E

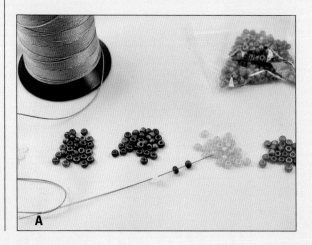

A

STRING ALL BEADS IN THE PATTERN

Always finish stringing all the beads in a sequence; don't stop halfway through a row. This is especially important if your piece uses an invisible join technique, an oft-used seamless join that will be covered later in the book.

If you've put on too many beads, you can always stop crocheting when you reach the desired length. Once you've cut your cord, however, you will have to join a new cord onto your old one to begin again if you need to add beads. When in doubt, don't cut your cord!

The project instructions list bead counts or give an estimate in grams so you know how many beads a project will require.

The bracelets shown in this book are sized to fit an average wrist: Bangles without clasps are about 7" (18cm) in circumference. If your target size is much smaller than average, stop crocheting before you reach the last of the beads strung and check the fit.

If your target size is much larger than average, add beads as you string. String entire repeats if the chart shows a pattern.

Always try to have more seed beads than you think you will need in case you misjudge how many beads it will take to complete your project.

Count your seed beads to be truly accurate. For example, if a design calls for 20 rows of 11º black beads and your pattern is 8-around: 8 x 20 = 160 black 11º seed beads for that pattern.

Where you begin crocheting will determine the "spin" of your piece—the natural diagonal formed by the crochet rope. If a pattern does not specify where to start or you are crocheting an easy pattern (using a bead "soup" or making a continuously repeating pattern), you can begin stringing your beads at the beginning of the pattern and crocheting with the first bead available (the last bead strung on the cord).

Right-handed vs. left-handed bead crochet

Bead crochet ropes naturally spiral because beads in subsequent rounds are offset half a bead width. Right-handed people hold the crochet hook in their right hand and the cord in their left hand, and they crochet in a counterclockwise direction.

Left-handed people hold the crochet hook in their dominant left hand, the cord in their right hand, and they crochet in a clockwise direction around the crochet rope. The leftie's spiral will spin opposite that of the right-handed crocheter.

Either way you work, as long as you are consistent in stringing your beads and you crochet in the same direction every time, your finished piece will be fine.

USING A BEAD SPINNER

When you're stringing beads for a project that has no stringing pattern, you can use a bead spinner (such as the Spin-N-Bead) to string beads onto the cord.

Basic slip-stitch method

HOLDING THE CORD

There are many ways to hold your cord, and you will develop your own preferences. I wrap the cord around my pinky finger once, take it under my ring and middle fingers, then wrap halfway around my index finger **[A]**. The cord that comes over the index finger is the tension cord, which controls how easily you catch the cord with the crochet hook, among other things. The cord looped around the pinky finger keeps the cord steady in your hands.

HOLDING THE HOOK

Right-handed crocheters will hold their cord in their left hand and the crochet hook in their right hand; left-handed crocheters will hold their cord in their right hand and the crochet hook in their left hand. With the tip of the hook pointed up and facing you, grasp the hook with your thumb and middle finger at the flat center and place your index finger about ⅛–¼" (3–6mm) behind the tip **[B]**. Let your remaining two fingers naturally curl inward toward your palm.

TIP All photos show a right-handed beader.

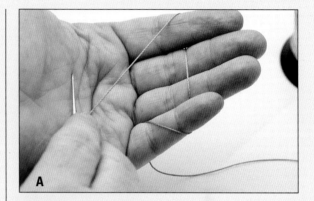

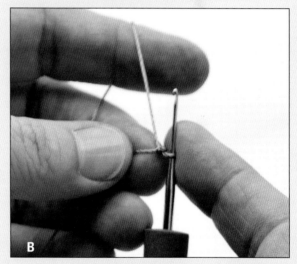

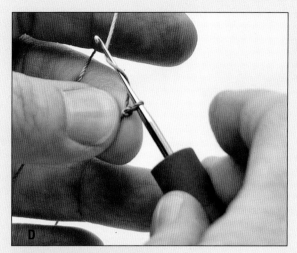

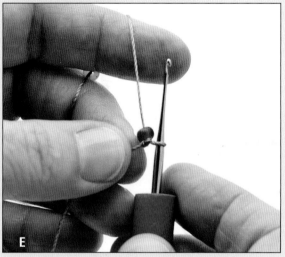

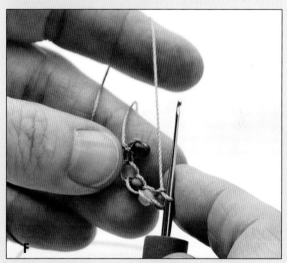

FIRST ROUND OF SLIP-STITCH

The first round of slip-stitch bead crochet is a beaded chain stitch. Each stitch contains one bead. The number of beads are how many "around" your rope pattern contains. For example: 5-around = 5 beads per round.

If you've never crocheted before, practice making a chain stitch without using beads first. Begin by making a slip knot **[C]**, leaving about a 12" (30cm) tail. The tail should be closest to you and the working cord farthest away from you. Hold the working cord (the cord with the beads on it).

Place your hook in front of the working cord, and with about 1" (2.5mm) of the hook sticking above the knot, loop the hook around the cord once **[D]**. Hooking the cord like this is called "yarning over." Pull the cord through the existing loop. This makes one chain. Continue until you are comfortable with this stitch, holding the chain with your thumb and middle finger. Hold your work with your thumb and index finger. Your left index finger controls the tension and serves as a "bead feeder." It helps to maintain your finger spacing at a

finger-width distance between the crochet rope and the cord, and to hold it straight to maintain the cord and bead position properly.

To begin a beaded chain stitch, make a slip knot as you did above, but slide a bead down onto the cord, atop your finger **[E]**. Allow the bead some room and capture the bead in a chain stitch using the same method as above.

Slide another bead down and yarn over. Pull through to complete the stitch. Continue in this manner until the first round of beads is crocheted. Flip the beads around so your hook is at the bottom, and the tail and first bead is at the top of your work. The chained beads will curve **[F]**.

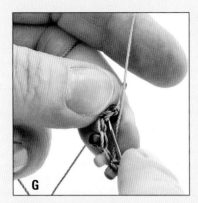

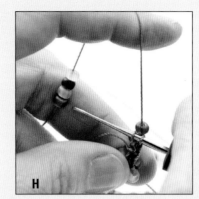

To close your beads in a circle forming the first round of your crochet rope **[G]**, slip the hook into the back V of the first beaded chain, yarn over, and complete a beadless stitch to close the chain. Be sure the tail is hanging down below your chain, and tug on it slightly while holding the beaded chain. The tail may want to move above your work (see "Troubleshooting," p. 18).

SECOND ROUND

Insert your hook in the first bead chain stitch to the left of the first bead (you may need to push this bead to the right). You should have two loops on your hook. Slide a bead down. For a simple spiral pattern as shown in Projects 1–3, the bead should be the same color as the bead underneath it in round 1. Hold the hook horizontal to help position the bead between the two loops **[H]**.

Yarn over, and pull the cord through both loops on the hook **[I]**. The bead just added should be standing upright, or vertical, and the bead below it should be horizontal. The top bead should be the same color as the bead below it, which is the first bead you crocheted. You have completed one bead stitch!

TIP You may need to pull the hook through one loop at a time at first until you become more experienced. This motion will become more fluid with time.

Proceed to the next bead and repeat: Insert the hook to the left of the next bead in the previous round and slide the next bead to the hook. Make sure it is the same color as the stitch the hook is inserted in. Yarn over, and pull the hook through both loops. Continue until you have added all the beads in the second round.

ROUND THREE AND BEYOND

At the beginning of round 3, your two previous rounds should become easier to see. Continue crocheting by concentrating on the steps: Insert the crochet hook to the left of the next bead. The working cord should be between the two loops, allowing the new bead to sit between the two loops. Slide the bead down, yarn over, and pull the cord through the two loops and over the previous row's bead.

When in doubt, focus on the color of the beads. The easy patterns of the first few projects provide a continuous "bead check" for you: Each new bead should go on top of the previous round's bead in the same color. If it doesn't match, you've made an error and will need to pull out a bead or two until you return to the correct pattern.

Continuing the rope

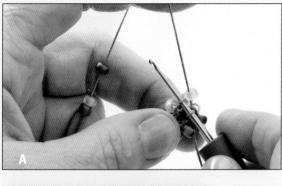

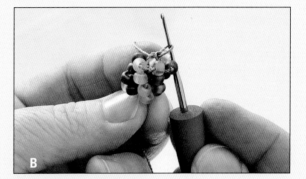

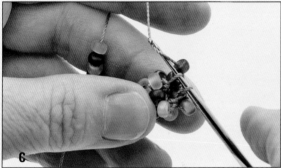

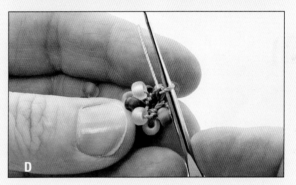

Do you have four or five rounds crocheted successfully? Congratulations! If you're having trouble, view the DVD again, review the starting techniques on the previous pages, and give it another try.

Here are some suggestions to help you move along as the crochet rope grows.

HOLDING THE ROPE AS YOU WORK

With your left hand (for right-handed people), hold the rope with your thumb and middle finger as you crochet. This takes practice, so don't get discouraged—it will come to you. Rotate the rope slightly clockwise to help position the cord properly as well, so you can see the rope side **[A]**. Tug on the working cord slightly and gently move the beads on the rope around to help form the rope shape in the first few rows.

The completed rounds will be horizontal and the round of beads that you've just finished crocheting (the most current round at the top) will stand up vertically. The "bead flip" makes the beads in the previous round sit horizontally. Note how the rope has a spiral design on the sides **[B]**. The order

in which the beads are strung determines how patterns are made. The inside of your rope will look rounded as you progress.

SLIDING BEADS DOWN THE WORKING CORD

At first it may be easier to slide one bead down the working cord at a time. But as you progress, you can slide several beads down, leaving the extra beads along the inside of your hand or across your index finger **[C, D]**.

CHECK THE LENGTH

The bracelets shown in this book are sized to fit an average wrist (they are about 7"/18cm in circumference). Always check the length of the crocheted part of your piece before the next step, which is adding the closure, and add or remove beads if necessary.

Necklace lengths are given in the instructions. If you want to increase or decrease the length substantially, take that into account as you string beads on the cord. Double-check the length after crocheting and before adding the closure.

Troubleshooting

Trouble getting started?
Solution: Try crocheting with larger beads, such as 5º seed beads or pony beads, to help you learn the basic stitch. Progress to 6º beads when you are comfortable.

No rope?
At about row 3, if you don't start to see a distinctive circle pattern forming when looking down into the rope, you may have crocheted the wrong bead into a stitch. It is very easy for the tail to move and cause you to lose the top/bottom orientation, allowing a bottom bead instead of a top-row bead to be crocheted and causing a jumbled mess!

Solutions: Place a thin coffee stirrer or your crochet hook inside the hole and gently shape the hole to help the beads sit properly. Also, use the coffee stirrer or a thin skewer as a guide, and crochet around it to help maintain the rope shape. You can also tape the tail in the downward position to help maintain the rope

orientation. After 5–10 rounds, you can remove it; the rope shape will be sufficiently formed to maintain the shape.

Tail still flipping up?
Solution: Use a heavy bead or weight tied with a slip knot to the tail, near the beginning of your work, to keep the tail oriented toward the bottom of the rope. Remove it after you've successfully crocheted 5–10 rows (or keep it in place).

Having difficulty yarning over?
Solution: Make sure the sizes of the cord and crochet hook are a good match. If the hook is too small for the cord (such as using a #11 crochet hook with a thick cord such as #34 C-Lon) it can cause problems.

Bead in the top row isn't sitting in a vertical position? Or you can't tell which bead to crochet because two of the same color are at the top?
Solution: This often happens because the cord went under the previous row's bead instead of over it. If you have a bead that sits inside the rope (the bead looks sunken into the rope and more cord is visible than with other beads), the cord hasn't cleared the bead properly. Try putting your pin into the rope and popping the bead out. If that doesn't work, you will need to unstitch the rounds until you reach the offending bead, and then begin crocheting again.

Beads aren't falling into their proper places?
Solutions: Position the cord between the two loops, keep your crochet hook horizontal, and keep your left hand's index finger straight and upright.

A thin coffee stirrer can help the beads sit properly.

A heavy bead or weight can keep the tail oriented to the bottom of the rope.

Here, the cord went under the previous row's bead instead of over it.

Technique 4

Finishing techniques

You can finish your bead crochet rope in several ways, and the closure choice will determine how you finish your last round. In general, you will need to either crochet the last group of beads without a bead, or stop when you've crocheted all your beads.

Before moving to the finishing steps, be sure the length of the crochet rope is right (allowing for the addition of the closure), and add or remove crocheted beads to adjust.

BEADLESS FINISH

If the finish for your bead crochet rope will use a focal bead, cones, bead caps, or fringe ends (basically every type of closure except the invisible join), use the following beadless finish before going on to attach your closures.

To finish the last row of beads in your crochet rope, continue crocheting your last group of beads beadless (with the cord only): For each stitch, insert the hook into the next stitch, yarn over without pulling a new bead down, and pull the hook through both loops **[A]**. This step will cause the last row of beads to lie horizontally **[B]**.

Pull the working cord through the last loop and, leaving a 12" (30cm) tail, cut the cord. By pulling the cord through the last loop, you'll prevent your work from unraveling. To further prevent the cord from working itself out of the loop, clip your working cord with a Bead Stopper or tie a slip knot in the cord.

You're now ready to add the closure and finish your piece.

FOCAL BEAD CLOSURE

Thread the tail onto a tapestry needle, string the focal bead on the needle **[C]**, and pass the needle through the middle of the other end of the crochet rope.

A

B

C

TIP Check the fit of the bracelet around your wrist or place the necklace around your neck before adding a closure and ending your piece.

Exit the rope 3–6 rounds from the end and between two cords **[D]**. Do not exit a bead or split a cord. Remove the tapestry needle, thread the remaining tail onto the needle, and pass it through the focal bead and through the middle of the other end of the crochet rope, 3–6 rounds from the end **[E]**. One tail should exit each section of the rope.

Snug up the ends so they touch the focal bead **[F]**. Secure the cord in your work with a half-hitch knot between beads **[figure, right]**, and pass the needle back through the center of the rope and through the focal bead. Snug up the end to the focal bead again and tie a half-hitch knot to secure the cord.

TIP

Focal beads for necklaces are finished in the same way as focal beads in bracelets. The beads can be further enhanced by using an accent seed bead color to make the focal piece stand out.

Pass back through the focal bead one more time for each cord. That will give you a total of six passes through the focal bead—plenty of cord to secure the work.

With the tapestry needle and cord, pass the needle further into the center of the rope, exiting the opposite side 3–6 beads further into the rope. Tie two more half-hitch knots and trim the cord, leaving a ½–1" (1.3–2.5cm) tail. Do the same for the remaining tail. Gently push the tails into the rope for a finished piece **[G]**.

LARIAT CLOSURE

Choose end beads to complement your piece. A flat bead cap that covers the end of the rope, along with large beads and crystals, are beautiful ways to turn a finished rope into a lariat.

Finish the last row of crochet with the beadless finish. Thread the tail onto a tapestry needle and slip the decorative beads on the cord.

Snug the beads to the end of the rope. String a small bead to act as a stopper. Go back through the decorative beads and bury the tail in the work just as you would for a focal closure, tying half-hitch knots in three different locations along the crochet rope. Trim the cord, leaving a ½–1" (1.3–2.5cm) tail, and gently push the tails into the rope.

Unlike the beads in the focal closure, the end beads aren't a pressure point in the work, so no extra passes are necessary.

CLASP CLOSURE

You can create a clasp closure with or without endcaps; the technique is the same.

If desired, choose endcaps large enough to cover the thickness of the bead crochet rope. Finish the last row of bead crochet with the beadless finish. Thread the tail on a tapestry needle and pass the needle and cord through the endcap (if using), exiting the smaller end. Gently push the cone or cap over the crochet rope end. Pass the needle and cord through a jump ring or the loop of a clasp **[H]**.

Pass the needle back through the endcap and into the center of the crochet rope, exiting 3–6 beads from the end of the rope between two cords. Secure the cord with a half-hitch knot between beads. Pass the needle back up through the center of the rope, through the endcap, and over the jump ring or clasp loop to secure to your work **[I]**. Pass back through the rope and down 3–6 beads into the work, exiting between two cords. Tie several half-hitch knots, and trim the cord (see Focal Bead Closure, p. 19).

It may be difficult to pass the cord through a small endcap opening a second time. If you run into this problem, pass through the endcap only twice. After passing through the opening the first time, loop your cord around the jump ring or clasp loop several times. Then pass the needle and cord down through the opening and finish using the regular focal closure method. The endcaps aren't a pressure point in your work, so no extra passes are necessary.

FRINGE CLOSURE

Fringe beads add movement to your crochet piece. Creating fun, dangle fringes requires a little knowledge of basic stringing and is similar to a lariat closure, but uses many more dangles.

Finish your last row of bead crochet with the beadless finish, p. 19. If you want to add endcaps and/or a focal bead, do it now (see earlier instructions).

For the fringe, use seed beads that match the beads in the bead crochet rope, or use complementary beads such as Czech fire-polished beads, metal beads, crystals, or a seed bead mix. Make the fringe as long or as short as you'd like.

Thread a beading needle with 2 yd. (1.8m) of beading cord such as 6 lb. test Fireline or B or D weight Nymo. Center the needle on the cord so the cord is doubled. Secure the cord in the rope using the same half-hitch and back-and-forth methods described earlier. Exiting along an edge on the end of the rope, pick up four to six fringe beads.

As with the lariat closure, end with a small seed bead and turn around. Skip the last small seed bead, and pass through the fringe beads up into the bead crochet rope. To reinforce, loop the cord around a stitch and pass back through all the fringe beads again. Continue until all your desired fringes are added. Use a half-hitch knot to tie off within the bead crochet rope. Trim the cord and hide the tail within the crochet rope.

INVISIBLE JOIN CLOSURE

To finish the last row of beads with an invisible join, do not crochet the last round of beads. Pull the working cord through the last bead's loop and, leaving a 12" (30cm) tail, cut your cord and secure it as described in Focal Bead Closure, p. 19. The invisible join's seamless look is predicated on finishing the last round when joining the two ends together.

Read more about the invisible join in Technique 6, p. 38.

5-around hibiscus flower bracelet

Your first bead crochet project uses large 6º seed beads in five colors. The large bead size will help you learn and feel comfortable with the technique before proceeding to smaller beads, thinner cord, and finer crochet hooks.

PATTERN 5-around

FINISH Focal bead closure

MATERIALS & TOOLS

- 8 grams size 6º seed beads in each of the following colors:
  orange matte AB
  opaque bone matte
  amethyst color-lined purple matte
  galvanized yellow gold
  silver-lined chartreuse matte

- Polymer clay focal bead

- C-Lon #18 nylon bead cord or equivalent

- Bead Crochet Toolkit

Refer to Techniques 1 & 2 for detailed instructions about stringing the beads and getting started crocheting. Watch the DVD to see the starting techniques in action.

STRINGING & CROCHETING

String the beads in a 5-bead sequence following the A, B, C, D, E pattern and reading the pattern from left to right. The 5-bead sequence equals one row (round). For an average-size, $7^1/_2$" (19.1cm) bracelet, string 62–67 rows, ending with a complete 5-bead pattern. Crochet using the basic slip-stitch method, p. 14.

SIZING & FINISHING

Check the bracelet for size before trimming the cord. Keep in mind the size of the focal bead and add or remove rounds if desired. Finish using the focal bead closure technique, p. 19, and tie off to end the project.

Sizing a bangle

It's especially important to size a bangle correctly so it's not too tight, but stays on your wrist. Too tight is better than too loose. Your bangle will roll onto your wrist and in no time will stretch a little. Don't force the bracelet over your wrist; gently roll it on. It will roll quite easily, which will put less stress on the piece.

Wrap a tape measure around the largest part of your hand while touching your thumb to your pinky finger (as though you're sliding on a bangle) to find the total desired length if you want a snug fit. For a slightly looser fit, add about ¼" (6mm). Remember to take into consideration your focal bead if it is large. As you crochet your piece, check the fit of the bracelet with your closure in mind. It's always easy to add more beads. If you've already cut the cord, you'll have to pull out a couple rows, add new cord, and then crochet to the desired length.

BEAD KEY

A orange matte AB

B opaque bone matte

C amethyst color-lined purple matte

D galvanized yellow-gold

E silver-lined chartreuse matte

STRINGING PATTERN

1A, 1B, 1C, 1D, 1E

PROJECT 2

6-around hibiscus flower bracelet

Like the first project, this bracelet uses large 6º seed beads and steps up to six colors per round. Working another project with large beads will give you more practice before you progress to more challenging projects.

PATTERN 6-around

FINISH Focal bead closure

MATERIALS & TOOLS

- 8 grams size 6º seed beads in each of the following colors:
  salmon opal gilt-lined
  paprika opaque
  terra cotta opaque
  dark amber/brick matte lined
  amethyst/dark blue matte lined
  vermillion matte metallic

- Polymer clay focal bead
- C-Lon #18 nylon bead cord or equivalent
- Bead Crochet Toolkit

Refer to Techniques 1 & 2 for detailed instructions about stringing the beads and getting started crocheting. Watch the DVD to see the starting techniques in action.

STRINGING & CROCHETING

String the beads in a 6-bead sequence following the A, B, C, D, E, F pattern. The 6-bead sequence equals one row (round). String on 62–67 rows for an average-size, 7½" (19.1cm) bracelet, ending with a complete 6-bead pattern. Crochet using the basic slip-stitch method, p. 14.

SIZING & FINISHING

Check the bracelet for size before trimming the cord. Keep in mind the size of the focal bead and add or remove rounds if needed. Finish using the focal bead closure technique, p. 19, and tie off to end the project.

BEAD KEY

A salmon opal gilt-lined

B paprika opaque

C terra cotta opaque

D dark amber/brick matte lined

E amethyst/dark blue matte lined

F vermillion matte metallic

STRINGING PATTERN

1A, 1B, 1C, 1D, 1E, 1F

sedona sunset bracelet

This project uses large beads and five beads per round, ranging in size from 6º seed beads to 8º seed beads. The mix of sizes creates a slight undulating effect. This project introduces a different closure technique.

PATTERN 5-around

FINISH Clasp closure

MATERIALS & TOOLS

- Seed beads:
  8 grams 6º in salmon opal gilt-lined
  8 grams 6º in vermillion matte metallic
  8 grams 6º in amethyst/dark blue matte lined
  6 grams 8º in dark amber/brick matte lined
  6 grams 8º in teal matte

- Closure: ball-and-snap clasp and **2** endcaps in antique bronze color

- Cord: C-Lon #18 nylon bead cord or equivalent

- Bead Crochet Toolkit

STRINGING & CROCHETING

String the beads in a 5-bead sequence following the A, B, C, D, E pattern. The 5-bead sequence equals one row (round). String 72 rows for an average-size, 7½" (19.1cm) bracelet, ending with a complete 5-bead pattern. Crochet using the basic slip-stitch method, p. 14.

The smaller 8º seed beads may become slightly buried under the adjacent 6º seed beads. Crochet slowly and use your roundnose pin to pop out the beads if you notice they are slightly indented.

SIZING & FINISHING

Check the bracelet size before cutting the cord. Keep the length of the clasp in mind and add or remove rounds if needed. Finish using the clasp closure technique (p. 21), but instead of using a jump ring between the cone and the clasp, pick up two Es both before and after picking up the clasp. Tie off to end the project.

TIP Seed beads vary in weight per gram because of their finishes; a 6º metallic bead weighs more than a 6º with a standard finish. My estimates are generous to be sure you have enough beads to finish the project at hand.

BEAD KEY

A 6º salmon opal gilt-lined

B 6º vermillion matte metallic

C 6º amethyst/dark blue matte lined

D 8º dark amber/brick matte lined

E 8º teal matte

STRINGING PATTERN

1A, 1B, 1C, 1D, 1E

bead-mix and single-color bracelets

Using five or six colors of beads in the first few projects helps you double-check your work. After you're comfortable with your technique, try using seed beads in a single color or a mix. Mixes are widely available and come in a variety of pleasing color palettes.

PATTERN 6-around

FINISH Focal bead closure

MATERIALS & TOOLS

- Seed beads:
  Solid color bracelet: 31–35 grams 6º seed beads, opaque dark lilac
  Mixed color bracelet: 31–35 grams 6º seed bead mix

- Lampwork glass focal bead, 10mm

- Cord: C-Lon or S-Lon #18 nylon bead cord or equivalent

- Bead Crochet Toolkit

STRINGING & CROCHETING

You don't need to be concerned about a stringing pattern for either project—simply string beads on the cord. To be sure you have enough beads to complete 62–70 rows of a 6-bead pattern, string at least 372 beads on your cord (6 x 62 = 372 beads). This is enough for an average-size bracelet.

Work a 6-around rope using the basic slip-stitch method, p. 14, until you reach a length that is shorter than the desired finished length by about 10mm (or the width of your focal bead).

SIZING & FINISHING

Check the bracelet size before trimming the cord. Finish using the focal bead closure technique, p. 19, and tie off to end the project.

Using the same technique, make the rope longer and create a stunning necklace.

PROJECT 5

fringe-closure bracelets

Most projects in this book use traditional closures such as focal beads, cones or endcaps, or invisible joins. These bracelets use the fringe closure method. Crocheted in 6-around using 8º beads (cat bracelet) and size 6º seed beads (carnelian bracelet), this closure is a pleasing way to focus on the unusual netsuke bead or faceted semiprecious carnelian beads.

PATTERN 6-around

FINISH Fringe closure

MATERIALS & TOOLS

Cat netsuke bracelet

- 30 grams (1 hank) 8º Czech cut seed beads in auburn/dark mauve
- Carved wood netsuke bead
- **7** 6–7 mm jasper beads

Carnelian bracelet

- 35 grams 6º seed bead mix
- 14–16mm round faceted carnelian bead
- **4–5** 10mm round and faceted carnelian beads
- **4** 5–8mm Czech beads

Both bracelets

- Cord: C-Lon #18 nylon bead cord
- Bead Crochet Toolkit
- Beading needle #10
- Fireline 6 lb. test

STRINGING & CROCHETING

You don't need to be concerned about a stringing pattern for either project—simply string beads on the cord. For the cat bracelet, string at least 504 8º seed beads (84 rows of 6). For the carnelian bracelet, string at least 420 6º seed beads (70 rows of 6).

For either bracelet, crochet a 6-around rope using the basic slip-stitch method, p. 14. Measure your focal bead and any accent beads, then subtract that measurement from the desired finished length. Crochet until you reach that target measurement.

SIZING & FINISHING

Check the bracelet size before trimming the cord, allowing for the size of the focal and accent beads.

Finish the last row by crocheting a beadless stitch for each of the 6 stitches in the last row. Pull the cord through the last loop and cut the cord, leaving a 12" (30cm) tail. The finishing technique used for these two bracelets is similar to the beadless finish and focal bead closure, p. 19.

Cat netsuke bracelet: Thread the tapestry needle onto the tail cord. Pick up a jasper bead and pass through the cat bead head to toe. Pass through the middle of the opposite section of the tube, exiting between two beads 3–6 rows in. Make a half-hitch knot close to the beadwork.

Thread the beginning tail through the cat bead and the jasper bead. Run the cord through the middle of the other end of the rope, exiting between two beads 3–6 rows in. Make a half-hitch knot close to the beadwork.

Run both cords through each side again if possible (as you would for a focal bead closure). If it is too tight a fit through the jasper bead, feed only one cord end through a second time.

To add fringe beads, thread a comfortable length of Fireline onto a #10 beading needle. Leaving a 6" (15cm) tail, tie a knot onto the center of one of the tube end's cord to secure. Feed the cord into an edge bead and make a stitch to secure the thread. Add 6–10 seed beads (the same beads used in the bracelet), a jasper bead, and an 8º seed bead. Skip the 8º seed bead just added and go back through the jasper bead and all the seed beads. Make another stitch, exit the next 8º seed bead on the edge of the rope, and make another fringe in the same way. Continue making fringe around the end of the rope. Tie off inside the beadwork to conceal the knot.

Carnelian bracelet: Finish just like the cat bracelet, but use a 14–16mm carnelian bead instead of the jasper bead and cat bead. Add fringe as desired: My bracelet's fringes have alternating carnelian beads and Czech beads at the ends.

PROJECT 6

bead-mix bracelet

For this bracelet, choose a bead mix that includes varying size beads. By design, this creates a bumpy pattern that's full of texture. Be sure to mix up the sizes as much as possible as you string the beads. You may need to use a fine-gauge long-eye needle (see p. 37) if you have tiny 15º seed beads in the mix.

STRINGING & CROCHETING

This bracelet uses a seed bead mix, so there is no stringing pattern to follow. String approximately 600 beads. Use the 8-around slip-stitch method, p. 14, to crochet the bracelet to the desired length.

SIZING & FINISHING

Check the bracelet for size before trimming the cord. Finish using the focal bead closure technique, p. 19, sewing through a 10mm bead, the pewter focal, and another 10mm bead as if they were a single bead.

PATTERN 8-around

FINISH Focal bead closure

MATERIALS & TOOLS

- 25 grams seed bead mix in varying sizes
- Cord: #20 100% Egyptian combed cotton cord or micro-weight nylon cord
- Pewter cat/fish focal bead
- **2** 10mm polymer clay beads
- Bead Crochet Toolkit
- Fine-gauge long-eye needle (optional)

beginner necklace

This is an excellent beginner necklace, as it uses a 6º seed bead mix. The challenge in making this piece is connecting the necklace sections through a long focal bead.

PATTERN 6-around

FINISH Clasp closure

MATERIALS & TOOLS

- 60 grams 6º seed beads in color to complement focal bead
- 35mm curved focal bead
- Clasp in sterling silver
- Cord: C-Lon #18 nylon bead cord
- Bead Crochet Toolkit

STRINGING & CROCHETING

This 17" (43cm) necklace uses a bead mix, so there is no stringing pattern to follow. String approximately 350 beads. Using the basic slip-stitch method, p. 14, work a 6-around sequence until the rope is about 6" (15cm). Work a beadless finish and cut the cord, leaving a 24" (61cm) tail. Repeat to make a second rope.

To connect the long focal bead, thread the long tail of one rope on the tapestry needle, and string seed beads to fit inside the focal bead. String as many beads as will fit in the focal bead without extending past the edges so they're not visible when the necklace is completed. String the focal bead over the seed beads.

Carefully pull the beads out of the focal bead while still on the tail. Thread the tapestry needle onto the long tail of the other bead crochet rope. Sew through the focal bead and the seed beads you just added onto the first tail. Gently pull both tails and the beads through the focal bead. Pass one cord through the center of the crochet rope, but don't tie a knot yet. Thread the tapestry needle on the other tail and repeat. Two cords should be going through the focal bead and the seed beads.

If you are going to wear your necklace quite a bit, you should consider running another pass through the focal bead with both tails as a precaution, especially if your focal bead is heavy. You don't need to run the cord through the seed beads in the focal bead. To prevent the cord from being seen, snug up your crochet rope so there are no cords showing and the rope is against the focal bead ends.

FINISHING

Slowly snug up all the cords and the crochet rope so there are no cords showing. Finish the tails as you would a focal bead closure. Finish the remaining ends using the clasp closure technique, p. 21, but pick up four seed beads before and after picking up the clasp.

PROJECT 8

summertime necklace

After you are comfortable with the basic bead crochet stitch, the Summertime Necklace is an excellent next-step project. While the project still uses large bead sizes, it also incorporates a row of 4mm pearls, adding a touch of elegance to the piece, as does the lovely magnetic clasp. *By Rifka Boswell*

PATTERN 7-around

FINISH Clasp closure

MATERIALS & TOOLS

- 16 grams 8º seed beads, white
- 26 grams 6º seed beads, white
- **154** 4mm Swarovski pearls, Powder Almond
- Magnetic two-piece clasp with rhinestones
- Cord: C-Lon or S-Lon #18 nylon bead cord or equivalent
- Bead Crochet Toolkit

Beads include 8°s, 6°s, and 4mm pearls. Using the varied bead sizes creates an undulating effect along the spiral. This necklace project builds skills in using pearls and gives you the opportunity to try using a new closure—a two-part magnetic clasp.

STRINGING & CROCHETING

String the pattern in a complete 7-bead sequence in the following order: four 8°s, a 6°, a 4mm Swarovski pearl, a 6°. Repeat for 154 rows.

TIP Follow the stringing order carefully to achieve the undulating effect.

BEAD KEY

A 8°, white

B 6°, white

C 4mm pearl, Powder Almond

The pearl is larger than the 6° seed bead, so this piece should be crocheted slightly loose—that is, the tension shouldn't be too tight to allow for each bead to be visible and not nestle inside the rope. To sit on top of the rope, the pearls require less tension than the seed beads. To encourage them to sit in the right place, insert the roundnose pin inside the crocheted tube and gently push the pearls out.

Using the basic slip-stitch method, p. 14, work a 7-around sequence until you have crocheted all the beads.

SIZING & FINISHING

Check the size before cutting the cord. As shown, this necklace is choker length (about 16"); add length if desired. Finish using the clasp closure technique, p. 21, and tie off to end the project.

STRINGING PATTERN

4A, 1B, 1C, 1B

Adjusting your tension

Having trouble getting your hook through the loops? You might be crocheting too tightly. Lighten up on your tension and see how much easier it is to get the hook through.

Try practicing with 6° beads, not making anything in particular, but concentrating on consistency and what is most comfortable for you. You control tension with your left hand and index finger while crocheting, so move your finger up or down to help adjust the cord. If you need to adjust the tension on the loops within your crochet rope, pull up slightly with the crochet hook. Additionally, push the hook up within the two loops while yarning over, forcing the cord down along the shaft of the hook every time to loosen the cord (a good practice for habitual tight crocheters).

Technique 5

Moving beyond the basics

As you move along in the book, you'll discover several key differences between beginner and more challenging projects.

Bead size. The size of the seed beads decrease. Generally, the projects will use 11º seed beads, a combination of 8ºs and 11ºs, or 15ºs. With the use of smaller beads, the patterns become more prominent showing flowers, diamonds, stripes, and crisscrosses. The combination of bead size and pattern will add visual interest to the pieces.

Cords. You'll find that these projects will use either a thin nylon cord or 100% cotton cord in either #20 or #40. (Refer to the Guide on p. 11 for more detailed information.) The thinner cords are more supple and allow for a nice drape in your jewelry.

Needles. When using 15º seed beads, you will need a thinner Big Eye-style needle. Fine-gauge Japanese bead needles are the perfect solution. I recommend the 9cm needle for bead crochet. While a little more costly than typical Big Eye needles, these last a very long time and are worth the investment (see Resources, p. 85).

Crochet hooks. The size of the hook becomes smaller, as the cord size decreases to obtain the specific patterns. Projects after this technique section use hooks that range from size 8 to 10. I usually use a size 9 crochet hook with 11º seed beads and size 14 with 15º beads.

USING A ROW COUNTER

While most beginner projects don't require a bead or row counter, it doesn't hurt to use one if you find yourself losing your place or having to recount your bead groups. However, row counting is absolutely necessary when making a project that uses patterns.

A kacha-kacha is a handy counter primarily used in the knitting community. To use it, simply zero out the counter and click once after stringing each row. This way you will always know which row you are on in your pattern.

Some people use a paper copy of the pattern and mark off each row strung. Others use a sticky note or a ruler, moving it down the pattern as they string.

Some people pick up small bits of paper after every row. For this method, cut very small pieces of paper, make a tiny hole using the roundnose pin. Pick up a piece of paper on the needle after each row of beads has been strung. Tear off the paper as you crochet.

Invisible join closure

A

B

The invisible join closure technique is the most challenging of all the closure methods. The seamless look is predicated on finishing the last round of beads manually as you join the ends. The last round of beads in the rope is left unfinished: as you begin the closure, the beads will be standing up vertically with the cord pulled through the last loop.

This method can be used with a slip-stitch bead crochet rope of any bead count diameter. The instructions that follow refer to a six-around rope, but if you make a five-around rope, for example, simply adjust the counts in the instructions accordingly.

Align the ends of the rope, holding the end you finished with on the left and the end you started with on the right **[A]**. The beads in the last round lie sideways to those in the previous round because they haven't been locked in place yet. Thread a tapestry needle on the tail from the starting end,

and sew into the center of the other end of the rope, exiting about four rows from the end **[B]**. Pull the ends of the rope near each other, but don't end the tail.

Identify the six beads added in the final round and the six beads in the first round. Here, the last bead added in the last round is dark brown and it sticks out from the rope a bit. At the starting end, the first bead that was crocheted is topaz and it also sticks out from the rope. When you align the ends, the first bead in the starting round will be next to the last bead in the ending round and the colors will form continuous spirals.

Remove the needle from the starting tail, and thread it onto the ending tail. Cross over to the starting end, and sew under the loop of the first bead (here, topaz), sewing from the inside of the rope to the outside of the rope **[C]**.
Cross over to the finishing end, and sew under the cord to

C

the right of the sixth bead from the end, flipping the bead as you would while crocheting **[D]**. Notice that this bead is the same color as the one your cord just came from at the other end (again, a topaz bead). Pull the cord to bring the ends close together.

Cross over to the starting end again and sew under the loop of the second bead from the end **[E]**.

Cross over to the finishing end, and sew under the cord to the right of the fifth bead from the end, flipping the bead as before **[F]**. Again, this bead is the same color as the one you just came from on the other end.

Continue working back and forth between the ends, flipping the beads in the final round and matching up the pattern. Rotate the rope and snug up the ends as you work. After you've flipped the last bead on the tail end, sew into the rope at the starting end, exiting several rounds from the end **[G]**.

To end the tails, sew in and out of the rope several times, crossing over the cord within the rope without sewing through any beads. Trim the cord as close to the beadwork as possible.

Technique 7
Too many or missing beads

As you're crocheting, frequently glance at your work to make sure the pattern is being crocheted properly. If you discover you have too many beads on your cord and your pattern is off, you have a few alternatives.

Crush the offending bead. This method, while the quickest, poses some risk as you can sever the cord by mistake (yes, I have done it several times). Insert a T-pin into the bead until it breaks. Or, with the T-pin in the bead to protect the cord, place the bead in the oval notch of a crimping pliers and gently crush it, covering it with your hand so pieces don't fly off and injure you.

Crochet the extra bead(s) into the center rope of your work. Start in the same spot you left off with the correct bead. If done correctly, you won't see the beads; they'll be inside the rope and you've made quick work of a potentially time-consuming task.

If you find you don't have enough beads or your pattern is incorrect and you simply have to restring the pattern section of beads, you have no choice but to cut the cord. Proceed to learning how to change cord (below) now!

Technique 8
Changing cord

You'll encounter a few good reasons to change cords when making bead crochet jewelry. The primary reason is missing beads in a pattern. Frequently one, two, or more beads have been left off your cord or misstrung.

When you discover you've missed some beads, the easiest solution is to cut your working cord and restring the pattern correctly.

After crocheting the last correct bead, keep your working cord's loop on the hook. Cut the working cord, leaving a 6–8" (15–20cm) tail. Pass the hook through the next loop to the left of the last bead added. This is where you will continue the pattern and add new cord.

Make a slip knot in the new working cord. Grab the loop with the crochet hook and tighten the loop on the hook. Pull the new cord through the loop of the old cord on the hook. To secure the new cord to your crochet rope, chain stitch several stitches inside the crochet rope, making your way around to the last bead added.

Your new bead should be the next bead in your pattern. Place the hook through the loop and continue crocheting as usual. After crocheting a few rows, secure the working cord with a locking stitch marker. Tie the two cord ends together inside the rope and clip the excess cord (a nylon cord zapper works well too). These tails will be contained inside the rope.

band of color bracelets

The Band of Color bracelets have always been my favorite "go-to" bracelet for everyday wear. Over the years I've created many combinations of complementary colors, with each color separated by a simple black band.

PATTERN 8-around

FINISH Invisible join

MATERIALS & TOOLS
Bracelet A (left)

- 6 grams 11º Japanese seed beads, black

- 3 grams 11º Japanese seed beads in each of **6** matte opaque colors: rose, pink, powder blue, gray, purple, cream

- Cord: #20 100% cotton crochet thread or C-Lon micro nylon bead cord

- Bead Crochet Toolkit

- Row Counting Tool

Bracelet B (right)

- 7 grams 11º Czech seed beads, matte black

- 4 grams 11º Czech seed beads in each of **6** colors: matte purple, metallic dark purple, metallic burgundy brown, purple-lined transparent gray, opaque light mahogany, light mahogany

- Cord: #20 100% cotton crochet thread or C-Lon micro bead cord

- Bead Crochet Toolkit

- Row Counting Tool

STRINGING & CROCHETING

The Band of Color Bracelet is a great skill-expanding project. This project requires counting not only the beads strung on your cord, but also the number of rows strung for each color band (see "Using a counter," p. 37).

String the pattern from left to right in complete 8-bead sequences. The 8-bead sequence equals one row. End with a complete 8-bead sequence: Don't end on bead 3 of 8 for example, as it will throw off your row count. Complete the rows so your join will be perfect.

This project will give you a taste of following a long graphic stringing pattern (shown starting on p. 43). Alternatively, you can follow the simple written stringing pattern for Bracelet A. It alternates eight rows of color with four rows of black. If you're feeling adventurous, create your own "bands of color" pattern.

Using the basic slip-stitch (p. 14), work in 8-around until all of the beads are used.

STRINGING PATTERN BRACELET A

8 rows of color A (64 beads)
4 rows of black (32 beads)
8 rows of color B (64 beads)
4 rows of black (32 beads)

Continue with eight rows of color C and so on. For an average-size breacelet, string the combination of eight rows of color with four rows of black nine or 10 times, alternating the six bead colors. Bracelet A (left bracelet) has 108 rows. Bracelet B (right bracelet) has 120 rows.

SIZING & FINISHING

It's easy to add a complete set of bands: a color band of eight rows (approximately ⅝"/1.6cm) and a black band of four rows approximately ¼" (6mm). Each set will add about ¾" (1.9cm) to the length.

Additionally, adding or omitting a row or two of color anywhere within your pattern is an easy way to slightly extend or shorten the size of the piece. Example: use seven or nine rows of color instead of eight.

Check the length before cutting the cord. Finish using the invisible join closure technique, p. 38, and tie off to end the piece. Connect a black row to a color row for the least-visible join.

TIP The difference between Japanese and Czech seed beads creates a slight difference in row count between the two bracelets. Bracelet A has nine bands of color and nine bands of black seed beads. Bracelet B, made with smaller Czech seed beads, has 10 bands of color and 10 black bands.

BEAD KEY
BRACELET A

- **A** matte rose
- **B** black
- **C** matte pink
- **D** matte powder blue
- **E** matte gray
- **F** matte purple
- **G** cream

STRINGING PATTERN
BRACELET A

8A	
8A	
8A	
8A	
8A	
8A	
8A	
Row 8	8A
8B	
8B	
8B	
Row 12	8B
8C	
8C	
8C	
8C	
8C	
8C	
8C	
Row 20	8C
8B	
8B	
8B	
Row 24	8B
8D	
8D	
8D	
8D	
8D	
8D	
8D	
Row 32	8D

8B	
8B	
8B	
Row 36	8B
8A	
8A	
8A	
8A	
8A	
8A	
8A	
Row 44	8A
8B	
8B	
8B	
Row 48	8B
8C	
8C	
8C	
8C	
8C	
8C	
8C	
Row 56	8C
8B	
8B	
8B	
Row 60	8B
8E	
8E	
8E	
8E	
8E	
8E	
8E	
Row 68	8E
8B	
8B	
8B	
Row 72	8B
8F	
8F	
8F	
8F	
8F	
8F	
8F	
Row 80	8F
8B	
8B	
8B	
Row 84	8B

8G	
8G	
8G	
8G	
8G	
8G	
8G	
Row 92	8G
8B	
8B	
8B	
Row 96	8B
8D	
8D	
8D	
8D	
8D	
8D	
8D	
Row 104	8D
8B	
8B	
8B	
Row 108	8B

43

STRINGING PATTERN
BRACELET B

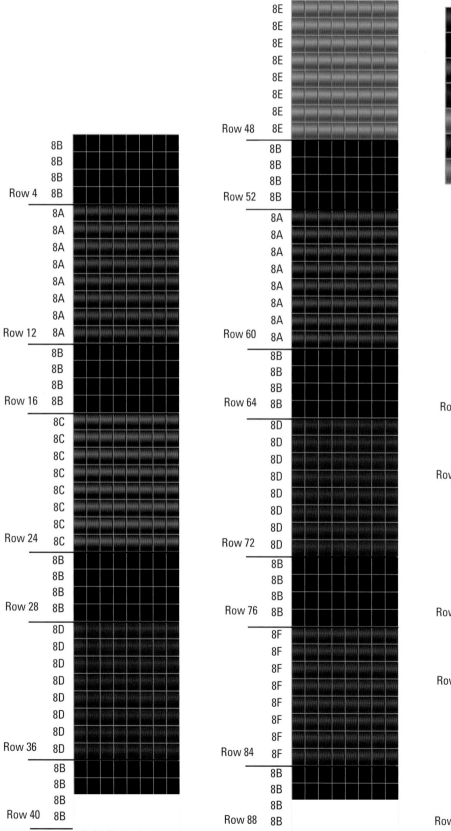

	8B
	8B
	8B
Row 4	8B
	8A
	8A
	8A
	8A
	8A
	8A
	8A
Row 12	8A
	8B
	8B
	8B
Row 16	8B
	8C
	8C
	8C
	8C
	8C
	8C
	8C
Row 24	8C
	8B
	8B
	8B
Row 28	8B
	8D
	8D
	8D
	8D
	8D
	8D
	8D
Row 36	8D
	8B
	8B
	8B
Row 40	8B

	8E
	8E
	8E
	8E
	8E
	8E
	8E
Row 48	8E
	8B
	8B
	8B
Row 52	8B
	8A
	8A
	8A
	8A
	8A
	8A
	8A
Row 60	8A
	8B
	8B
	8B
Row 64	8B
	8D
	8D
	8D
	8D
	8D
	8D
	8D
Row 72	8D
	8B
	8B
	8B
Row 76	8B
	8F
	8F
	8F
	8F
	8F
	8F
	8F
Row 84	8F
	8B
	8B
	8B
Row 88	8B

	8G
	8G
	8G
	8G
	8G
	8G
	8G
Row 96	8G
	8B
	8B
	8B
Row 100	8B
	8D
	8D
	8D
	8D
	8D
	8D
	8D
Row 108	8D
	8B
	8B
	8B
Row 112	8B
	8E
	8E
	8E
	8E
	8E
	8E
	8E
Row 120	8E

BEAD KEY
BRACELET B

A purple opaque matte

B black matte

C metallic dark purple

D metallic burgundy brown

E purple-lined transparent gray

F opaque light mahogany

G light mahogany

PROJECT 10

twist bracelets

The Twist Bracelet is a good pattern to try after you've made several bracelets. It uses 8º and 11º seed beads with 15º seed beads to create an exaggerated, undulating twist.

The second twist bracelet is made with 8º and 11º seed beads and 11º cylinder beads in similar coppery colors. Use matte and metallic beads of the same color next to each other, and add light copper-color cylinders to further highlight the twist.

PATTERN 8-around

FINISH Invisible join

MATERIALS & TOOLS

Bracelet A (left)
- 8 grams 8º seed beads, light peach opal gilt-lined
- 5 grams 11º seed beads, matte metallic brown (457B)
- 5 grams 15º seed beads, Toho 557 gold
- 3 grams 11º seed beads, rose gold luster

Bracelet B (right)
- 9 grams 8º seed beads, 460A (plum or cabernet matte metallic)
- 5 grams 11º seed beads, plum copper metallic, 457C
- 4 grams 11º Delica cylinder beads, copper PF, color 40

Both bracelets:
- Cord: #40 100% cotton thread
- Bead Crochet Toolkit
- Row counting tool

STRINGING & CROCHETING

String the pattern from left to right in complete 8-bead sequences for 120–130 rows. The 8-bead sequence equals one row.

Using the basic slip-stitch (p. 14), work in 8-around until all of the beads are used.

BEAD KEY
BRACELET A

A 15º seed beads, gold

B 11º seed beads, matte metallic brown

C 8º seed beads, light peach opal gilt-lined

D 11º seed beads, rose gold luster

STRINGING PATTERN
BRACELET A

3A, 2B, 2C, 1D

End with a complete 8-bead sequence to allow for an invisible join.

SIZING & FINISHING

Check the length before cutting the cord. Finish using the invisible join closure technique, p. 38, and tie off to end the piece.

BEAD KEY
BRACELET B

A 8º seed beads, plum or cabernet matte metallic

B 11º seed beads, plum copper metallic

C 11º cylinder beads, copper

STRINGING PATTERN
BRACELET B

3C, 2B, 2A, 1B

tie dye reverse spiral bracelet

Elegance and style describe this bracelet. The Tie Dye Reverse Spiral Bracelet incorporates several colors of 8º seed beads, 11º seed beads, and 11º cylinder beads. The reversing colors created by intersecting lines of 8ºs with patches of complementary colors in both 11º seed beads and the smaller 11º Delicas create a sophicated palette. *By Linda Lehman*

PATTERN 8-around

FINISH Invisible join

MATERIALS & TOOLS

- 4 grams 8º seed beads in each of **4** colors: matte gray, gunmetal, matte black, and metallic dark gold
- 6 grams 11º seed beads in each of **2** colors: white Ceylon luster and metallic gunmetal brown
- 5 grams 11º Delica cylinder beads, gold metallic
- Cord: #20 100% cotton crochet thread or C-Lon micro bead cord
- Bead Crochet Toolkit
- Row counting tool

This pattern requires concentration as you string beads on the cord. Refer to "Using a counter," p. 37; it is important to count bead rows carefully so the bracelet has the correct shape.

STRINGING & CROCHETING
String your bead patterns from left to right, stringing entire 18-row sets of beads.

The bracelet shown has 7 sets of 18 rows and is approximately 5¾" (14.6cm) in diameter (small-to-average wrist size).

Using the basic slip-stitch (p. 14), work in 8-around until all of the beads are used.

Each set of 18 rows equals about ⅞" (2.2cm) in length. To lengthen, increase by a complete set of 18 rows.

SIZING & FINISHING
Before you cut the cord, check the fit. Add or remove 18 rows at a time to maintain the pattern.

Finish using the invisible join closure technique, p. 38, paying close attention to which 11º seed bead colors you are joining. Tie off to end the work.

BEAD KEY

A 8º seed bead in matte gray

B 8º seed bead in gunmetal

C 11º seed bead in white ceylon luster

D 11º Delica bead in gold metallic

E 11º seed bead in metallic gunmetal brown

F 8º seed bead in matte black

G 8º seed bead in metallic dark gold

How many bobbins?
A typical bracelet pattern will fill up one medium size bobbin or sometimes two.

It's wise to string and crochet no more than this at one time: Friction caused by the beads passing over the cord in the crocheting process can fray the cord, eventually breaking it. Too many beads will weaken the cord. Also, too long a cord becomes unmanageable, becoming tangled and knotted.

String and crochet necklaces in separate sections: String about the same number of beads as you would for a bracelet, and crochet each part of the pattern separately. Use the invisible join technique, p. 38, to join the sections.

STRINGING PATTERN

1A, 1B, 1A, 2C, 3D	
1E, 1A, 1B, 1A, 1C, 3D	
2E, 1A, 1B, 1A, 3D	
3E, 1A, 1B, 1A, 2D	
Row 5	3E, 1C, 1A, 1B, 1A, 1D
	3E, 2C, 1A, 1B, 1A
	3E, 2C, 1D, 1A, 1B
	1F, 2E, 2C, 2D, 1A
	1G, 1F, 1E, 2C, 3D
Row 10	1F, 1G, 1F, 2C, 3D
	1E, 1F, 1G, 1F, 1C, 3D
	2E, 1F, 1G, 1F, 3D
	3E, 1F, 1G, 1F, 2D
	3E, 1C, 1F, 1G, 1F, 1D
Row 15	3E, 2C, 1F, 1G, 1F
	3E, 2C, 1D, 1F, 1G
	1A, 2E, 2C, 2D, 1F
Row 18	1B, 1A, 1E, 2C, 3D

Technique 9

Using crystals and daggers

Using crystals and dagger shapes adds elegance and interest that's hard to achieve with seed beads alone. However, crystals have sharp edges that can cut through cotton cords, and the movement of dagger beads can fray cord quickly if you wear your piece often. You have several options when crocheting with these types of beads.

For size 4mm and smaller crystals and dagger beads: Fine-weight nylon cords such as fine-weight C-Lon are good for smaller beads (11ºs and 15ºs) and come in many colors. They don't break as easily as cotton cord.

Reinforce daggers and crystals with Fireline on a beading needle after you have finished crocheting. This is particularly important if you used cotton thread for crocheting. Make a knot at the beginning and end of the reinforcement, and tie half-hitch knots at various points in the beadwork if you have many daggers.

TIP

Reinforce crystals and daggers at any point that gets constant friction, such as around the neck, around the wrist, and at closure points. Daggers and crystals in a no-stress zone such as in lariat ends may not need the extra thread. My rule? If in doubt, reinforce!

For pieces with large crystals, use a heavyweight nylon cord (as recommended for size 6º seed beads in the chart on p. 11).

PROJECT 12

crystal band bracelet

Crystals lend an elegance to an already lovely bracelet, and this pattern combines both a single-row band of crystals with a spiral of two or three seed bead colors in the rope. It's the perfect project to build your skills, as it uses 11º seed beads, but the stringing pattern isn't too complicated.

PATTERN 8-around

FINISH invisible join

MATERIALS & TOOLS

Colors are for topaz mix bracelet, right

- **80–90** 4mm Swarovski bicone crystals in the following color mix: Padparadscha Satin, Air Opal AB2x, Copper, Opal AB2x, Burgundy, Burgundy AB, Padparadscha Satin AB2X, Red Magma, Indian Red, Golden Shadow

- 8 grams 11º seed beads, silver-lined gold

- 6 grams 11º seed beads, silver-lined dark topaz

- Cord: #20 100% cotton crochet cord or C-Lon Micro cord

- Bead Crochet Toolkit

- Row counting tool

Two similar bracelets are shown on the left. The colors and instructions here are for the 8-around topaz version. (The other bracelet, a slight variation on this pattern, uses a 9-around pattern and three colors of seed beads.) This project is perfect for the bead crocheter who is becoming comfortable using 11° seed beads.

STRINGING & CROCHETING

I used rounds and bicones in my 4mm crystal mix. The crystals in this piece do not seem to cause any cord breakage. However, as with any piece using crystals, you may want to reinforce the rounds of crystals with Fireline.

Following the pattern, string entire 11-row sets from left to right. Using the basic slip-stitch (p. 14), work in 8-around until all of the beads are used.

End with a complete 11-bead sequence to allow for an invisible join.

String 10 sets of 11 rows for an average-size bracelet. Each additional 11-row set will add ¾" (1.9cm) to the length of the rope.

Note that the crystals take up more room on your bracelet than seed beads, so you'll have fewer rows overall than in an all-seed-bead bracelet.

SIZING & FINISHING

Check the fit before cutting the cord. Finish using the invisible join closure technique, p. 38, paying attention to which 11° seed bead colors you are joining. Each color should be joined to the same color on the opposite end of the piece. Tie off to end the piece.

BEAD KEY

 A 4mm crystal mix

B 11° seed beads, silver-lined gold

C 11° seed beads, silver-lined dark topaz

STRINGING PATTERN

8A	
5C, 3B	
5C, 3B	
5C, 3B	
5C, 3B	
5C, 3B	
5C, 3B	
5C, 3B	
5C, 3B	
5C, 3B	
Row 11 5C, 3B	

crystal twist bracelet

Incorporating crystals into bead crochet gives extra zing and sparkle to your pieces. The Crystal Twist Bracelet pattern uses 4mm Swarovski bicones and 8º and 11º seed beads to emphasize the twist. An interesting option would be to substitute 4mm Czech fire-polished beads for the 4mm bicones.

PATTERN 8-around

FINISH invisible join

MATERIALS & TOOLS

- 3 grams 8º seed beads, silver
- 4 grams 11º seed beads, silver
- 6 grams 11º seed beads, silver-lined pink
- **118** 4 mm Swarovski bicone crystals, Amethyst AB2x
- Cord: #20 100% cotton crochet cord or C-Lon micro cord
- Bead Crochet Toolkit
- Row counting tool

STRINGING & CROCHETING

String the beads in an 8-bead sequence following the pattern. The 8-bead sequence equals one row (round). String 118 rows for an average-size bracelet, ending with a complete 8-bead pattern. Crochet in 8-around basic slip-stitch, p. 14.

SIZING & FINISHING

Check the fit before cutting the cord, and add or remove rounds if desired. Finish using the invisible join closure technique, p. 38, and tie off to end the piece.

In my experience, the crystals in this piece do not seem to cause any cord damage, but you may want to reinforce the line of crystals with Fireline.

BEAD KEY

A 8º silver

B 11º silver

C 11º silver lined pink

D 4mm Amethyst AB2X

STRINGING PATTERN

1A, 2B, 4C, 1D

red velvet crystal necklace

Don't be surprised if you get stopped by complete strangers on a regular basis when you wear this necklace. The designer likes to pair it with black and white attire—and red lipstick, of course! *By Leila Martin*

PATTERN 4-around

FINISH Clasp closure with endcaps

MATERIALS & TOOLS

- Strand (13"/33cm) 4mm Red Velvet Chinese crystal rondelle beads
- Strand (13"/33cm) 6mm Red Velvet Chinese crystal rondelle beads
- **2** strands (13"/33cm each) 8mm Red Velvet Chinese crystal rondelle beads
- Strand (8"/20cm) 10mm Red Velvet Chinese crystal rondelle beads
- S-Lon bead cord
- **2** cones
- **4** 5mm jump rings
- Clasp
- Bead Crochet Toolkit
- Row counting tool

TIP

Stringing this necklace takes longer than crocheting it! Make it today and wear it tonight: The entire project took me less than 2 hours to complete.

STRINGING & CROCHETING

String half of the 4mm strand, half of the 6mm strand, an entire 8mm strand, the entire 10mm strand, another entire 8mm strand, the remaining half-strand of 6mms, and the remaining half-strand of 4mms.

Design options

It can be difficult to find beads in the same color in graduated sizes. But you can still make stunning jewelry with whatever crystal rondelles you find.
- Make a graduated necklace with a few similar colors.
- Use fewer different sizes.
- Try a 3-around version (more thread will show) or a 5-around version (chunky and fun!). After the crystals are strung, you can easily pull out your stitches and restart with a different count around.

Crochet in 4-around basic slip-stitch, p. 14, until the rope is about 17" or the desired length (less the cones and clasp).

SIZING & FINISHING

Finish using the clasp closure technique, p. 21.

TIP

It's best to finish the whole necklace in one sitting. The beads are heavy and even if you set it down for a moment, the weight of the beads may pull and cause several inches to unravel in a split second.

PROJECT 15

wire closure bracelets

Bracelets don't always need a focal bead or invisible join closure. These fashionable bracelets use memory wire and a wire cuff with ball ends as an armature, with pearls and crystals for some flair and flash. *By Rifka Boswell*

PATTERN 8-around

FINISH Specialty

MATERIALS & TOOLS

Bracelet A (pink and mauve)
- 15 grams 11º seed bead mix, pinks and mauves
- **10–12** 3–4mm Swarovski crystal mix in Purple AB, Amethyst AB, Rose, Light Amethyst, Light Amethyst AB
- 6" (15cm) 2.5 mm cuff bracelet with 6mm twist-off ball ends

Both bracelets
- Fireline 6 lb. test
- #10 beading needle
- Bead Crochet Toolkit
- Row counting tool

Bracelet B (white)
- 15 grams size 11º seed beads, opaque white
- **14–18** 3–4mm Swarovski crystal mix in Amethyst AB, Rose, Light Amethyst, Light Amethyst AB
- **2–4** 6mm Swarovski pearls, lavender
- **16–22** 1½" (3.8cm) steel headpins
- 12–14" (30–36cm) memory wire
- Heavy-duty wire cutters for memory wire
- Roundnose pliers

BALL-END BRACELET (A)

Bracelet A is formed around a ball-end wire cuff blank. One ball end unscrews and comes off so you can string the bead crochet rope onto it.

For bracelet A: String about 880 11º seed beads (enough for 110 rounds). Crochet in 8-around using basic slip stitch, p. 14.

Carefully slip the crochet rope onto the wire, being careful not to snag or puncture the beadwork. You may have to gently nudge it. The rope should sit on the wire and should not be bunched up or leave too much of a gap at either end. Bunching up the rope will cause the ends to continuously push up against the closure. Allow ½" (1.3cm) on each end for the crystal fringe and ball ends.

Adjust the rope's length to fit the wire cuff length. Sew 10 fringe dangles on each end with Fireline using the fringe closure technique, p. 21. For each fringe, string a 4mm or 6mm bicone crystal and an 11º seed bead, and sew back through the crystal into the end round of the crochet rope. Feel free to improvise to create different dangles!

MEMORY WIRE BRACELET WITH FRINGE (B)

Use memory-wire cutters to cut the wire to the desired length, allowing ½" (1.3cm) on each end to make a loop. Keep in mind that the bracelet will have some overlap, so trim the wire and plan your crochet rope length accordingly. If in doubt, leave the wire longer than you think you need it to be. You can trim it later if needed.

String about 960 11º seed beads (120 rounds). Crochet in 8-around using basic slip-stitch, p. 14. As with the ball-end bracelet, carefully slip the crochet rope onto the wire, being cautious to not snag or puncture your piece. You may have to gently nudge it on. The rope should sit on the wire and should not be bunched up or have too much of a gap at either end.

Measure the length, allowing ¾–1½" (1.9–3.8cm) for finishing (including the wire loop), depending on the amount of dangles you plan to add. Remove the beadwork from the wire. If necessary, adjust the length of the rope to fit the bracelet length as well. When the rope is the right length, work a beadless finish, p. 19.

At one end of the memory wire, make a loop using roundnose pliers. String a 6mm pearl, an 8mm pearl, the crochet rope, an 8mm, and a 6mm. Make a loop at the remaining end of the wire.

Sew eight fringe dangles on with Fireline using the fringe closure technique, p. 21. The fringe shown is made with a 4–6mm bicone crystal and a 15º seed bead. Attach two headpin dangles (see below) to each loop closure.

Headpin Dangles

String a 15º seed bead and a 4 or 6mm crystal on a headpin. Using chainnose pliers, hold the headpin above the bead. Use your fingers to bend the wire above the pliers at a right angle. Using roundnose pliers, hold the wire at the bend and gently curve the end of the wire around the top jaw of the pliers to make a loop, repositioning the pliers as needed so the wire makes a complete circle. String the dangle onto the loop at the end of the bracelet. Wrap the end of the wire around the wire stem between the loop and the bead. Trim the excess wire.

Technique

Pattern samplers

Patterns give you infinite possibilities for achieving movement, shape, and color combinations in your bead crochet jewelry. Working with more complex patterns requires you to count beads and rows carefully so the design turns out like you want it to. Flowers, triangles, stripes, and more allow you to plan challenging projects. As a bonus, you can use up small bead stashes!

Use a bead/row counting device such as a kacha-kacha or small bits of paper (see p. 37) to track your stringing progress. One bead forgotten or too many in a row will throw off a pattern, and you may need to eliminate or add beads to correct misstringings. It's easier to simply avoid a mistake in the first place.

The following five common patterns can be strung using the same spool of cord and are designed to give you practice in stringing patterns. Each uses a main color and just a few others that can be gathered from your bits of seed beads lying around.

My samplers are 25–30 rounds each. String repeats of the complete sequences to create the patterns shown and work 8-around using the basic slip-stich, p. 14.

To make a bracelet from one of the patterns, repeat the pattern as many times as you need to equal approximately 120 rounds. If desired, combine patterns in a single piece. Try using a base of 11º seed beads with 8's as accents to see what you get. Or try using white for the base beads and many colors for the accent beads.

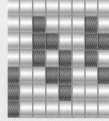

DIAMOND PATTERN BEAD KEY

A 11º seed bead, opaque white

B 11º seed bead, pink

STRINGING PATTERN

String left to right in complete repeats of the 7-row pattern and work in 8-around.

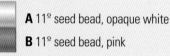

8A
2A, 1B, 3A, 1B, 1A
2A, 2B, 2A, 2B
2A, 1B, 1A, 1B, 1A, 1B, 1A
1B, 2A, 2B, 2A, 1B
1B, 3A, 1B, 3A
1B, 7A

STRIPES PATTERN BEAD KEY

A 11º seed bead, opaque white

B 11º seed bead, pink

STRINGING PATTERN

String left to right in complete repeats of the 8-bead sequence and work in 8-around.

1B, 1A, 1B, 1A, 1B,
1A, 1B, 1A

S PATTERN BEAD KEY

A 11º seed bead, opaque white
B 11º seed bead, blue

STRINGING PATTERN

String left to right in complete repeats of the 6-row pattern and work in 8-around.

```
              8A
  2B, 2A, 2B, 2A
1A, 1B, 3A, 1B, 2A
1A, 1B, 3A, 1B, 2A
1A, 1B, 3A, 1B, 2A
1A, 2B, 2A, 2B, 1A
```

DOTS PATTERN BEAD KEY

A 11º seed bead, opaque white
B 11º seed bead, blue

STRINGING PATTERN

8-around, for 30 rows. String from left to right, top to bottom.

```
                        8A
1A, 1B, 1A, 1B, 1A, 1B, 1A, 1B
```

FLOWERS PATTERN BEAD KEY

A 11º seed bead, opaque white
B 11º seed bead, blue
C 11º seed bead, black
D 11º seed bead, red

STRINGING PATTERN

String left to right in complete repeats of the 25-row pattern and work in 6-around.

```
                      6A
             2A, 2B, 2A
         2A, 1B, 1C, 1B, 1A
             3A, 2B, 1A
Row 5                 6A
             1A, 2D, 3A
         1A, 1D, 1C, 1D, 2A
             2A, 2D, 2A
                      6A
Row 10                6A
                 2B, 4A
         1B, 1C, 1B, 3A
             1A, 2B, 3A
                 5A, 1D
Row 15       1D, 4A, 1D
             1C, 1D, 4A
                 2D, 4A
                      6A
                 4A, 2B
Row 20       4A, 1B, 1C
             1B, 4A, 1B
                 1B, 5A
             3A, 2D, 1A
         3A, 1D, 1C, 1D
Row 25           4A, 2D
```

triangle bracelet

Stringing alternating sets of six and seven 11°s with 8°s and drops creates the edges and sides of the Triangle Bracelet. Here, 11°s in three bright contrasting colors are used for the sides. You can turn the bracelet inside out to change the play of colors—one color will always be hidden inside. *By Yoshie Marubashi*

PATTERN START 6-around

FINISH Invisible join

MATERIALS & TOOLS

- **87** 4x6mm Czech pressed glass drop beads, Jet AB
- 3 grams 8° seed beads, matte orange
- 3 grams 11° seed beads, opaque black
- 3 grams 11° seed beads, opaque pale sky blue
- 3 grams 11° seed beads, opaque orange
- Cord: #20 100% cotton crochet thread or C-Lon Micro cord
- Bead Crochet Toolkit
- Row counting tool

STRINGING & CROCHETING

When you string the same number of beads for each round, the bead crochet work forms a spiral because the beads are offset by a half-bead space. In this pattern, you will alternate between 7-bead and 6-bead rounds to create a straight pattern instead of a spiral.

Review the strung beads every few rows to be sure you have the correct count in order to create the shape of the edges and sides.

A dramatic alternative would be to use longer magatama beads or even daggers to further define the edges.

Following the pattern, string beads from left to right in complete repeats of the 4-row pattern. String 29 sets of the 4-row pattern for an average-size bracelet, ending with a complete pattern. Crochet in basic slip-stitch, p. 14, starting with a chain of six beads and alternating between 7- and 6-around as you continue.

SIZING & FINISHING

Check the fit before cutting the cord. Add or remove complete 4-row sets if desired (one set is about ⅜"/1cm). Finish using the invisible join closure technique, p. 38, matching each color to the same color on the opposite end of the rope. Tie off to end the piece.

BEAD KEY

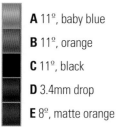

A 11º, baby blue

B 11º, orange

C 11º, black

D 3.4mm drop

E 8º, matte orange

STRINGING PATTERN

String left to right for 116 rows (29 sets of 4).

2A, 2B, 2C, 1A	
1A, 1D, 1B, 1D, 1C, 1D	
2A, 2B, 2C, 1A	
Row 4 1A, 1E, 1B, 1E, 1C, 1E	

PROJECT 17

square bracelet

Bead crochet can have four sides! Like Yoshie's Triangle Bracelet, this Square Bracelet design offers another unusual colorway and shape. Here she uses alternating bead counts and inserts drop beads and 8º's on the edges. The sides are 11º's in four bright colors, and the bracelet can be rolled to show off a different color each time you wear it. *By Yoshie Marubashi*

PATTERN START 9-around

FINISH Invisible join

MATERIALS & TOOLS

- **116–136** 3.4mm Czech pressed glass drop beads, transparent peridot
- 8 grams 8º seed beads, opaque spring green
- 3 grams 11º seed beads, yellow green lined transparent lime green
- 3 grams 11º seed beads, silver-lined lemon yellow
- 3 grams 11º seed beads, silver-lined matte plum
- 3 grams 11º seed beads, silver-lined matte red
- Cord: #20 100% cotton crochet cord or C-Lon Micro cord
- Bead Crochet Toolkit
- Row counting tool

STRINGING & CROCHETING

More beads per round are involved in this bracelet than the Triangle Bracelet—nine beads for the first and third rows and eight for the second and fourth rows. Adding a bead every two rows creates a straight line in this design rather than the usual bead crochet spiral.

Following the pattern, string beads from left to right in complete repeats of the 4-row pattern. String 29 sets of the 4-row pattern for an average-size bracelet, ending with a complete pattern.

Crochet in basic slip-stitch, p. 14, starting with a chain of 8 beads and alternating between 9- and 8-around as you continue.

SIZING & FINISHING

Check the fit before cutting the cord. Add or remove complete 4-row sets if desired (one set is about ⅜"/1cm). Finish using the invisible join closure technique, p. 38, matching each color to the same color on the opposite end of the rope. Tie off to end the piece.

BEAD KEY

A 11º seed bead, silver-lined matte red
B 11º seed bead, silver-lined matte plum
C 11º seed bead, yellow-green lined transparent lime green
D 11º seed bead, silver-lined lemon yellow
E 8º seed bead, opaque spring green
F 3.4 mm drop bead, peridot color

STRINGING PATTERN

String left to right for 116 rows (29 sets of 4).

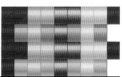

2A, 2C, 2B, 2D, 1A
1A, 1F, 1C, 1F, 1B, 1F, 1D, 1F
2A, 2C, 2B, 2D, 1A
Row 4 1A, 1E, 1C, 1E, 1B, 1E, 1C, 1E

PROJECT 18

versatile pattern bracelets

These sampler patterns are perfect bead crochet projects. All of the samples are worked in basic slip-stitch and finished with an invisible join. Any of the bracelet patterns can easily be turned into thin necklace ropes. *By Yoshie Marubashi*

yellow rose

PATTERN 6-around

FINISH Invisible join

MATERIALS & TOOLS

- 5 grams 11º seed beads, opaque maroon
- 3 grams 11º seed beads, yellow
- 1 gram 11º seed beads, silver-lined green
- 2 grams 11º seed beads, transparent light green
- 1 gram 11º seed beads, pink
- Cord: #20 100% cotton crochet cord or size C-Lon Micro cord
- Bead Crochet Toolkit
- Row counting tool

BEAD KEY

A 11º seed beads, opaque maroon

B 11º seed beads, yellow

C 11º seed beads, silver-lined green

D 11º seed beads, transparent light green

E 11º seed beads, pink

STRINGING PATTERN

String 11 sets of 12 rows for a total of 132 rows for an average-size bracelet.

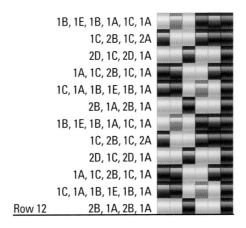

1B, 1E, 1B, 1A, 1C, 1A	
1C, 2B, 1C, 2A	
2D, 1C, 2D, 1A	
1A, 1C, 2B, 1C, 1A	
1C, 1A, 1B, 1E, 1B, 1A	
2B, 1A, 2B, 1A	
1B, 1E, 1B, 1A, 1C, 1A	
1C, 2B, 1C, 2A	
2D, 1C, 2D, 1A	
1A, 1C, 2B, 1C, 1A	
1C, 1A, 1B, 1E, 1B, 1A	
Row 12 2B, 1A, 2B, 1A	

PATTERN 9-around

FINISH Invisible join

MATERIALS & TOOLS

- 10 grams 11º seed beads, black
- 3 grams 11º seed beads, white
- 3 grams 11º seed beads, orange
- Cord: #20 100% cotton crochet thread or C-Lon Micro cord
- Bead Crochet Toolkit
- Row counting tool

tribal design

BEAD KEY

A 11º seed beads, black

B 11º seed beads, orange

C 11º seed beads, white

STRINGING PATTERN

String 6 repeats of the 19-row pattern for a total of 114 rows for an average-size bracelet.

2B, 1A, 1C, 5A	
1B, 1A, 1B, 6A	
1B, 2A, 1B, 2A, 1C, 2A	
1B, 1A, 1C, 1A, 1B, 1A, 2C, 1A	
1B, 1A, 2C, 1A, 1B, 1A, 1C, 1A	
1B, 2A, 1C, 2A, 1B, 2A	
1B, 6A, 1B, 1A	
1B, 1A, 1C, 3A, 1C, 1A, 1B	
1B, 1A, 2C, 2A, 2C, 1A	
Row 10 — 2B, 1A, 1C, 3A, 1C, 1A	
1B, 1A, 1B, 6A	
1B, 2A, 1B, 2A, 1C, 2A	
1B, 1A, 1C, 1A, 1B, 1A, 2C, 1A	
1B, 1A, 2C, 1A, 1B, 1A, 1C, 1A	
1B, 2A, 1C, 2A, 1B, 2A	
1B, 6A, 1B, 1A	
1B, 5A, 1C, 1A, 1B	
1B, 1A, 1C, 3A, 2C, 1A	
Row 19 — 1B, 1A, 2C, 3A, 1C, 1A	

chrysanthemum

Small drop beads are highlights in the focal flowers in this pattern. With a simple change of color palette, you can create a cool leopard look (see parentheses in materials list).

BEAD KEY

A 11º seed beads, opaque yellow
B 11º seed beads, blue-green
C 11º seed beads, transparent light green
D 3mm drop beads, clear
E 11º seed beads, pink

MATERIALS & TOOLS

- 10 grams 11º seed beads, blue-green (brown)

- 6 grams 11º seed beads, opaque yellow (gold)

- 4 grams 11º seed beads, transparent light green (black)

- 4 grams 11º seed beads, pink (tan)

- **16** clear 3mm drop beads (yellow)

- Cord: #20 100% cotton crochet thread or C-Lon Micro cord

- Bead Crochet Toolkit

- Row counting tool

STRINGING PATTERN

String 16 repeats of the 8-row pattern for a total of 112 rows for an average-size bracelet.

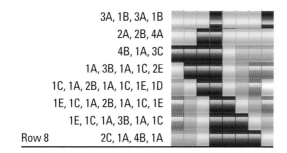

3A, 1B, 3A, 1B	
2A, 2B, 4A	
4B, 1A, 3C	
1A, 3B, 1A, 1C, 2E	
1C, 1A, 2B, 1A, 1C, 1E, 1D	
1E, 1C, 1A, 2B, 1A, 1C, 1E	
1E, 1C, 1A, 3B, 1A, 1C	
Row 8	2C, 1A, 4B, 1A

MATERIALS & TOOLS

- 16 grams 11º seed beads, translucent gray
- 4 grams 8º seed beads, opaque red
- 1 gram 11º seed beads, opaque yellow
- **32** 7x10mm leaf beads or drop beads, green
- Cord: C-Lon Micro cord
- #10 beading needle
- Fireline 6 lb. test
- Bead Crochet Toolkit
- Row counting tool

red camellia

BEAD KEY

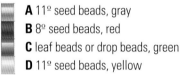

A 11º seed beads, gray
B 8º seed beads, red
C leaf beads or drop beads, green
D 11º seed beads, yellow

STRINGING PATTERN

String 14 repeats of the 9-row pattern for a total of 126 rows for an average-size bracelet. After crocheting, reinforce the leaf beads with Fireline. Embellish the rope with a few addition leaf beads, if desired.

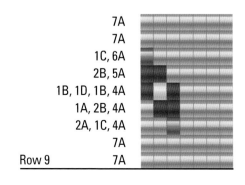

	7A
	7A
	1C, 6A
	2B, 5A
	1B, 1D, 1B, 4A
	1A, 2B, 4A
	2A, 1C, 4A
	7A
Row 9	7A

PROJECT 19

zigzag necklace

This is the perfect necklace for using up all your leftover 11° seed beads. Use black, white, and any colors you love. You may be surprised by how simple the stringing pattern is! *By Yoshie Marubashi*

PATTERN 8-around

FINISH Clasp closure

MATERIALS & TOOLS

- 5 grams 11º seed beads, black
- 10 grams 11º seed beads, opaque white
- 1 gram each 11º seed beads in up to 42 colors
- **2** 8mm accent beads
- Cord: #20 100% cotton crochet thread or C-Lon Micro cord
- Bead Crochet Toolkit
- Row counting tool

Each pattern set is made up of two sections that create the zigzag pattern. Each section has 11 rows and consists of a band of color that is interrupted by a black-and-white stripe. Each section is a different color. You can repeat each color as often as you wish or select a different color for each section.

SECTION 1 STRINGING PATTERN

For section 1 of each set, string 5 colored 11º seed beads, 1 white, 1 black, and 1 white. Repeat the pattern 10 times.

SECTION 2 STRINGING PATTERN

For section 2 of each set, string 6 colored beads, 1 white, 1 black, and 1 white. Repeat the pattern 10 times.

Continue stringing two-section sets (22 rows), choosing a different color for each section, until you have 21 sets (for a 30"/76cm necklace). String more or fewer sets to adjust the length. Work in 8-around basic slip-stich, p. 14, until you've used all the beads or the rope is the desired length. Finish with a clasp closure technique, p. 21, adding an 8mm accent bead at each end of the rope if desired.

PROJECT 20

petite patterns bracelet

This bracelet uses small seed beads—11º cylinders and 11º seed beads. The resulting rope is scaled down and delicate. Pay close attention to the stringing pattern, which appears a bit more random than those in previous projects. The bracelet on the left shows a variation with drops added.

PATTERN 6-around

FINISH Invisible join

MATERIALS & TOOLS

- 8 grams 11º Delica beads, color-lined rainbow juicy red (DB1780)
- 4 grams 11º Delica beads, transparent orange (DB703)
- 9 grams 11º seed beads, robin's egg blue
- 9 grams 11º seed beads, green-lined transparent chartreuse AB
- 9 grams 11º seed beads, transparent yellow

- 5 grams 11º seed beads, transparent light citrine-lined crystal clear
- 2 grams 11º seed beads, black
- 5 black 3 mm drops (optional)
- **47** 3 mm drops in various complementary colors (optional)
- Cord: #40 cotton
- Bead Crochet Toolkit
- Row counting tool

STRINGING & CROCHETING

String beads according to the pattern for an average-size bracelet. If desired, substitute 3mm drop beads in matching colors at various points in the pattern to add interest and movement to the bracelet (shown in the variation on the previous page).

To increase the size of the bracelet, string an additional 3–4 rows anywhere there is a color with one black bead per row. A good rule of thumb for size 11º seed beads is 4 rows = 1/4" (6mm) and 15 rows = 1" (2.5cm). You could also add rows to the black bands, but don't string more than 3 or 4 rows of black beads at a time, as they will overpower the design.

Count rows and check the pattern frequently.

Using the basic slip-stitch (p. 14), work in 6-around until all of the beads are used.

FINISHING

Finish using the invisible join closure technique, p. 38.

BEAD KEY

A 11º seed bead, red
B 11º seed bead, orange
C 11º seed bead, black
D 11º seed bead, blue
E 11º seed bead, green
F 11º seed bead, yellow
G 11º seed bead, crystal

STRINGING PATTERN

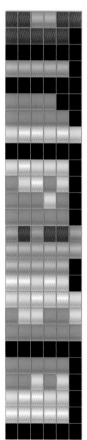

12 rows: 2A, 2B, 2A
10 rows: 5A, 1C
2 rows: 6C
11 rows: 5D, 1C
1 row: 6C
8 rows: 4E, 2C
1 row: 5E, 1C
5 rows: 1F, 2G, 1F, 1G, 1F
1 row: 6C
1 row: 1F, 1G, 3F, 1C
1 row: 1E, 1F, 1G, 1E, 1F, 1C
1 row: 3E, 1F, 1E, 1C
7 rows: 5E, 1C
10 rows: 1B, 1A, 1B, 2A, 1B
3 rows: 6D
5 rows: 5D, 1C
5 rows: 2G, 1F, 1G, 1F, 1C
2 rows: 2F, 1G, 1F, 1G, 1F
2 rows: 1E, 2F, 2E, 1F
6 rows: 6E
3 rows: 6C
1 row: 5E, 1C
1 row: 2E, 1F, 1E, 1F, 1C
7 rows: 1F, 2G, 2F, 1C
7 rows: 5G, 1C
3 rows: 6C

peyote-inspired bracelet

This project was inspired by peyote-stitched bangles. The bracelet is a slightly thicker bracelet of 12-around. It requires no inside support because the pattern's bead placement creates a structure that is quite firm, much more so than typical rope-style bracelets.

PATTERN 12-around

FINISH Invisible join

MATERIALS & TOOLS

- 13 grams 11º seed beads, blue
- 2.5 grams 11º seed beads in silver
- 2 grams 11º seed beads in gold
- 1.5 grams 11º seed beads in white opaque
- 2.5 grams 8º seed beads in silver
- 2.5 grams 8º seed beads in gold
- **24** 4mm Swarovski crystals in Turquoise AB2X
- **12** 3mm Swarovski crystals in Montana blue AB2X
- **16** 3mm Swarovski crystals, Golden Crystal AB
- **12** 4mm Swarovski crystal pearls, Vintage Gold
- **12** 4mm Swarovski crystal pearls, Dark Teal Blue
- Cord: #20 cotton thread
- Bead Crochet Toolkit
- Row counting tool

Correct stringing is very important in this project to keep the rows of pearl ridges consistent. You can adjust the pattern length to fit your wrist measurements.

This pattern is reversible—just roll the bracelet on your wrist with the crystals on the outside and the pearls to the inside.

STRINGING & CROCHETING

String the beads following the pattern, *beginning with row 125 and work back to row 1*. Read the pattern from left to right, *from bottom to top*.

SIZING & FINISHING

This pattern is designed to allow a flexible end section for sizing. Add or remove complete rows to adjust the length. Use the invisible join closure technique, p. 38, to finish.

BEAD KEY

A 11º seed bead, blue

B 11º seed bead, silver

C 11º seed bead, gold

D 11º seed bead, white

E 8º seed bead, silver

F 8º seed bead, gold

G 4mm crystal, Turquoise AB2X

H 3mm crystal, Montana Blue AB2X

J 3mm crystal, Golden Shadow AB

K 4mm crystal pearl, Vintage Gold

L 4mm crystal pearl, Dark Teal Blue

STRINGING PATTERN

	12C
	1B, 1G, 6B, 1G, 2B, 1C
	12B
	1G, 6B, 1G, 4B
Row 5	12B
	6B, 1G, 5B
	9C, 2B, 1G
	6A, 1K, 1A, 4C
	1A, 1F, 8A, 1H, 1A
Row 10	4A, 1C, 2A, 1E, 4A
	1F, 8A, 1C, 2A
	3A, 1K, 2A, 1E, 5A
	8A, 1H, 3A
	2A, 1C, 2A, 1E, 5A, 1F
Row 15	7A, 1C, 4A
	1A, 1K, 2A, 1E, 5A, 1F, 1A
	6A, 1H, 5A
	1C, 2A, 1E, 5A, 1F, 2A
	5A, 1C, 6A
Row 20	2A, 1E, 5A, 1F, 3A
	4A, 1H, 6A, 1K
	1A, 1E, 5A, 1F, 4A
	3A, 1C, 6A, 1C, 1A
	1E, 5A, 1F, 5A
Row 25	2A, 1H, 6A, 1K, 2A
	5A, 1F, 6A
	1A, 1C, 6A, 1C, 2A, 1E
	1A, 1G, 2A, 1F, 7A
	1H, 6A, 1K, 2A, 1E, 1A
Row 30	3A, 1F, 8A
	6A, 1C, 2A, 1E, 2A
	2A, 1F, 8A, 1C
	5A, 1K, 2A, 1E, 3A
	1A, 1F, 8A, 1H, 1A
Row 35	4A, 1C, 2A, 1E, 4A
	1F, 8A, 1C, 2A
	1A, 1G, 1A, 1K, 2A, 1E, 5A
	8A, 1H, 3A
	2A, 1C, 2A, 1E, 5A, 1F
Row 40	7A, 1C, 4A

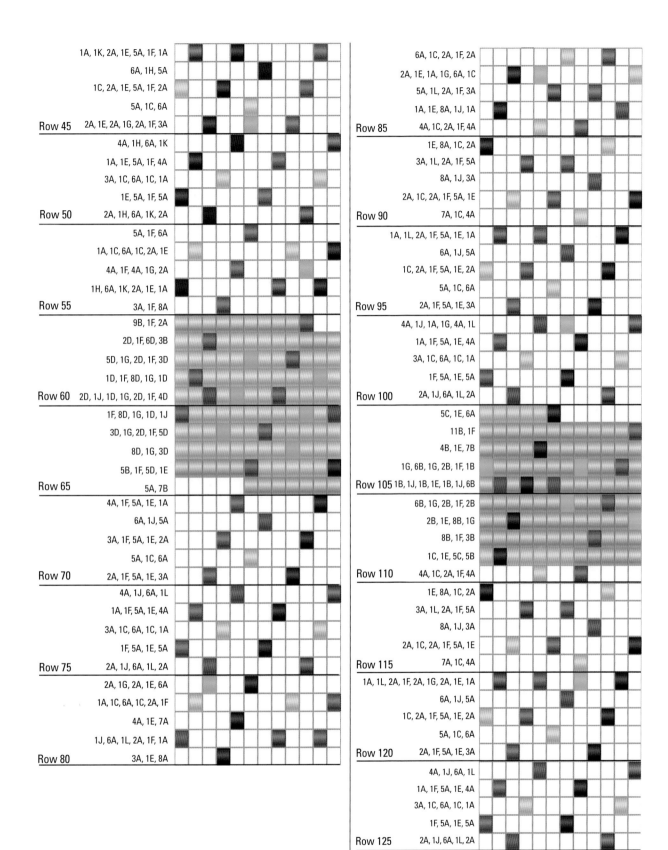

1A, 1K, 2A, 1E, 5A, 1F, 1A
6A, 1H, 5A
1C, 2A, 1E, 5A, 1F, 2A
5A, 1C, 6A
Row 45   2A, 1E, 2A, 1G, 2A, 1F, 3A
4A, 1H, 6A, 1K
1A, 1E, 5A, 1F, 4A
3A, 1C, 6A, 1C, 1A
1E, 5A, 1F, 5A
Row 50   2A, 1H, 6A, 1K, 2A
5A, 1F, 6A
1A, 1C, 6A, 1C, 2A, 1E
4A, 1F, 4A, 1G, 2A
1H, 6A, 1K, 2A, 1E, 1A
Row 55   3A, 1F, 8A
9B, 1F, 2A
2D, 1F, 6D, 3B
5D, 1G, 2D, 1F, 3D
1D, 1F, 8D, 1G, 1D
Row 60   2D, 1J, 1D, 1G, 2D, 1F, 4D
1F, 8D, 1G, 1D, 1J
3D, 1G, 2D, 1F, 5D
8D, 1G, 3D
5B, 1F, 5D, 1E
Row 65   5A, 7B
4A, 1F, 5A, 1E, 1A
6A, 1J, 5A
3A, 1F, 5A, 1E, 2A
5A, 1C, 6A
Row 70   2A, 1F, 5A, 1E, 3A
4A, 1J, 6A, 1L
1A, 1F, 5A, 1E, 4A
3A, 1C, 6A, 1C, 1A
1F, 5A, 1E, 5A
Row 75   2A, 1J, 6A, 1L, 2A
2A, 1G, 2A, 1E, 6A
1A, 1C, 6A, 1C, 2A, 1F
4A, 1E, 7A
1J, 6A, 1L, 2A, 1F, 1A
Row 80   3A, 1E, 8A

6A, 1C, 2A, 1F, 2A
2A, 1E, 1A, 1G, 6A, 1C
5A, 1L, 2A, 1F, 3A
1A, 1E, 8A, 1J, 1A
Row 85   4A, 1C, 2A, 1F, 4A
1E, 8A, 1C, 2A
3A, 1L, 2A, 1F, 5A
8A, 1J, 3A
2A, 1C, 2A, 1F, 5A, 1E
Row 90   7A, 1C, 4A
1A, 1L, 2A, 1F, 5A, 1E, 1A
6A, 1J, 5A
1C, 2A, 1F, 5A, 1E, 2A
5A, 1C, 6A
Row 95   2A, 1F, 5A, 1E, 3A
4A, 1J, 1A, 1G, 4A, 1L
1A, 1F, 5A, 1E, 4A
3A, 1C, 6A, 1C, 1A
1F, 5A, 1E, 5A
Row 100   2A, 1J, 6A, 1L, 2A
5C, 1E, 6A
11B, 1F
4B, 1E, 7B
1G, 6B, 1G, 2B, 1F, 1B
Row 105   1B, 1J, 1B, 1E, 1B, 1J, 6B
6B, 1G, 2B, 1F, 2B
2B, 1E, 8B, 1G
8B, 1F, 3B
1C, 1E, 5C, 5B
Row 110   4A, 1C, 2A, 1F, 4A
1E, 8A, 1C, 2A
3A, 1L, 2A, 1F, 5A
8A, 1J, 3A
2A, 1C, 2A, 1F, 5A, 1E
Row 115   7A, 1C, 4A
1A, 1L, 2A, 1F, 2A, 1G, 2A, 1E, 1A
6A, 1J, 5A
1C, 2A, 1F, 5A, 1E, 2A
5A, 1C, 6A
Row 120   2A, 1F, 5A, 1E, 3A
4A, 1J, 6A, 1L
1A, 1F, 5A, 1E, 4A
3A, 1C, 6A, 1C, 1A
1F, 5A, 1E, 5A
Row 125   2A, 1J, 6A, 1L, 2A

PROJECT 22

ruffles and spirals necklace

This project will expand your skills further with crocheted ruffles, caps, and endcaps.

PATTERN 8- and 10-around

FINISH Specialty

MATERIALS & TOOLS

- **225** 3mm Swarovski bicone crystals, Metallic Blue AB2x
- **250** 4mm Czech fire-polish beads, Black AB
- Cord: #40 100% cotton
- Bead Crochet Toolkit
- Row counting tool

This project will teach you how to create a nubby texture on a traditionally smooth bead crochet base—what I call ruffles. It uses increasing and decreasing bead counts within your work, adding cord, using smaller hooks, and seamlessly joining sections to form this designer necklace. You'll also learn many other crochet techniques unique to this design.

This piece has increases from 8- to 10-around and, as with many necklaces, this one is best crocheted in separate sections and connected. Therefore, each section's stringing directions are separated and numbered within that particular section. Feel free to split your sections up differently than what is suggested here.

CROCHETING

Throughout the ruffles and end caps sections in this project, you will crochet one beadless chain stitch after each ruffle stitch **[figure 1]**. This extra beadless stitch crocheted between each stitch on the ruffles row creates a loop to crochet into in the next round. (Without this beadless stitch, it would be difficult to work the ruffles because of the tightness of the work.)

Crochet the ruffle row into the previous row's beads as you would crochet any row. Place your hook into the left side of the bead, flip it over to the right **[A]**, then wrap the cord around the hook and pull it through the two loops **[B and C]**. Use loose tension to give the three or five beads in the ruffle stitch enough cord so they don't pull tightly.

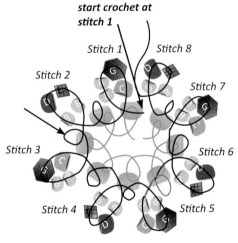

start crochet at stitch 1

Stitch 1 Stitch 8
Stitch 2
Stitch 7
Stitch 3 Stitch 6
Stitch 4 Stitch 5

Fig. 1

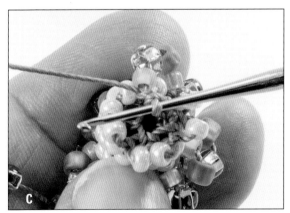

Work an extra chain stitch without a bead after each loopy stitch inserting the hook prior to the next bead **[D]**, yarn over and pull through **[E]**. If you don't add this unbeaded stitch between loops, you run the risk of unraveling your previous row's stitch.

CONNECTING THE SECTIONS

When you've finished crocheting a ruffles section, you can end the section and continue to (or connect to) the next section in one of two ways.

Option 1: Cut and pull the cord through the last loop. Work the next section separately and then connect the completed sections with an invisible join.

Option 2: Simply continue crocheting: Make a slip knot with the new cord, and using the crochet hook, pull the loop through the last stitch or loop of the previous section, just as though you are adding cord. To secure the new cord, crochet a few stitches inside the rope, circling back to the last bead on the previous section. Begin crocheting new beads onto the last bead of the previous section. (Essentially it's as if you never stopped crocheting; the join should not be evident.)

If you are joining the sections with different counts (i.e. 8-around in ruffles and 10-around in spirals), the join or continuation between the sections won't be a direct 1-to-1 relationship. Connect the sections evenly by skipping a stitch in the ruffles section after your stitches in the spiral section.

ENDCAPS & RUFFLES

This is the first section crocheted. Start stringing at the bottom of the piece (the endcaps) and continue by stringing the ruffles section.

The ruffles section alternates between a ruffle row and a band section (consisting of 4 rows of 8 beads) for a total of 17 ruffle rows and 17 band sections. Crochet starting with the ruffles and ending with the endcaps. You will make two of these endcaps & ruffles sections, each about 6" long.

After you've crocheted the last stitch of your endcap, pull the cord through the last loop and cut the cord, leaving a 12" tail. Weave the tail through the beadwork and make a half-hitch knot. Repeat twice, alternating sides (similar to tying off when using the focal bead closure). Trim the excess cord close to the work and gently pull the thread inside the work.

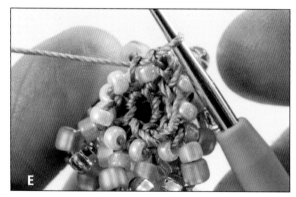

GUIDE TO THE NECKLACE SECTIONS

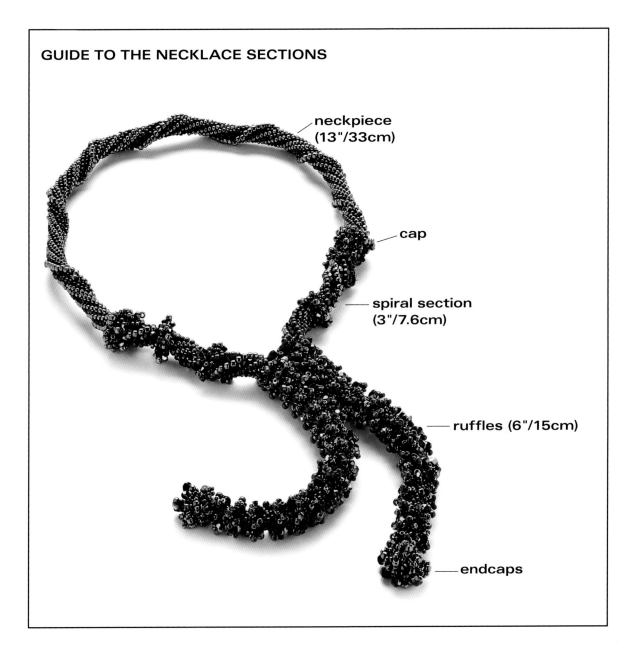

neckpiece (13"/33cm)

cap

spiral section (3"/7.6cm)

ruffles (6"/15cm)

endcaps

The graphs for this project look different than the other graphs in this book. For the rows made up of ruffles, each line represents a **single stitch**. So, a round of ruffles with eight stitches will be represented by eight lines of beads. The rows that don't have ruffles are represented like all the other graphs in the book—all the beads for the row are on a single line.

Begin stringing endcaps with Row 4. After stringing all the beads for the endcaps, string all the beads for the "ruffles" section starting with Row 5 of the first ruffle group. Continue stringing the "ruffles" section until all the beads are strung.

ENDCAP STRINGING PATTERN

String the first four rows of the endcap section.

RUFFLES STRINGING PATTERN

Each blue band section consists of four rows of eight beads each (32A total) and one ruffle row. A ruffle row is made of eight different stitches. String a total of 17 sets of bands and ruffles.

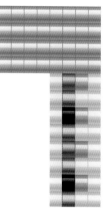

Row 5 =8A
Row 4 =8A
Row 3 =8A
Row 2 =8A
Row 1, Stitch 8 = 1B, 1F, 1D, 1B
Stitch 7 = 1C, 1G, 2B,
Stitch 6 = 1B, 1E, 1D, 1B
Stitch 5 = 1C, 1G, 2B
Stitch 4 = 1B, 1F, 1D, 1B
Stitch 3 = 1C, 1G, 2B
Stitch 2 = 1B, 1E, 1D, 2B
Stitch 1 = 1C, 1G, 2B

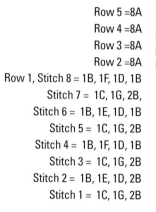

BEAD KEY

A 11º seed beads matte metallic blue

B 11º seed beads metallic bronze

C 8º seed beads matte metallic blue

D 8º seed beads metallic bronze

E 3mm bicones, Jet AB

F 3mm bicones, Metallic Blue AB2x

G 4mm Czech firepolished beads Black AB

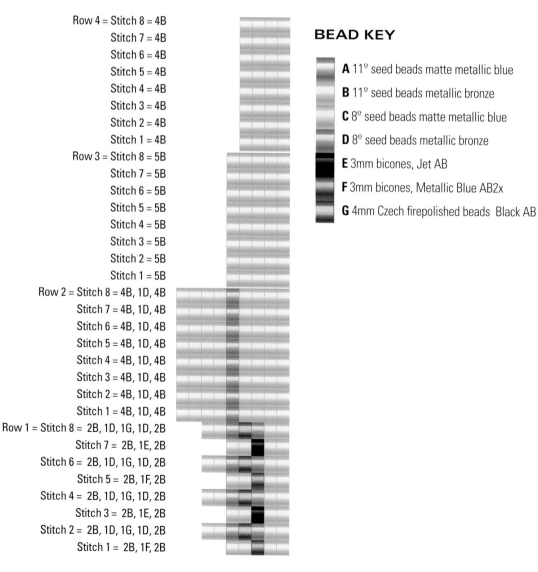

Row 4 = Stitch 8 = 4B
Stitch 7 = 4B
Stitch 6 = 4B
Stitch 5 = 4B
Stitch 4 = 4B
Stitch 3 = 4B
Stitch 2 = 4B
Stitch 1 = 4B
Row 3 = Stitch 8 = 5B
Stitch 7 = 5B
Stitch 6 = 5B
Stitch 5 = 5B
Stitch 4 = 5B
Stitch 3 = 5B
Stitch 2 = 5B
Stitch 1 = 5B
Row 2 = Stitch 8 = 4B, 1D, 4B
Stitch 7 = 4B, 1D, 4B
Stitch 6 = 4B, 1D, 4B
Stitch 5 = 4B, 1D, 4B
Stitch 4 = 4B, 1D, 4B
Stitch 3 = 4B, 1D, 4B
Stitch 2 = 4B, 1D, 4B
Stitch 1 = 4B, 1D, 4B
Row 1 = Stitch 8 = 2B, 1D, 1G, 1D, 2B
Stitch 7 = 2B, 1E, 2B
Stitch 6 = 2B, 1D, 1G, 1D, 2B
Stitch 5 = 2B, 1F, 2B
Stitch 4 = 2B, 1D, 1G, 1D, 2B
Stitch 3 = 2B, 1E, 2B
Stitch 2 = 2B, 1D, 1G, 1D, 2B
Stitch 1 = 2B, 1F, 2B

SPIRAL SECTIONS

The spiral section is a 10-around pattern. Each row has two crystals, and each of the three ruffles rows have both crystals and Czech fire-polish beads. You'll make two spiral sections.

The spiral section is slightly less complicated to crochet than the ruffles and cap sections, but you will face a new challenge: tension control! The size and shape of each bead plays a part in the extreme spiraling effect created by the bead combinations.

To prevent beads from disappearing within the rope as much as possible, take your time crocheting this section. Try for consistent even tension within this section. Check your tension and beadwork frequently to ensure all the beads are showing. Pay particular attention to vertical bead rows before and after the 8º seed beads and 3mm crystals. Tension that is too tight will bury the small beads underneath larger ones, and the vertical twist and flow of beads will be broken. Use a roundnose pin or tapestry needle to gently go underneath sunken beads and push them up and out.

The spiral section will connect to the ruffles section on one end and the long, smooth neckpiece section on the other. Crochet the spiral section without adding any of the neckpiece beads. Connecting at the top ruffles section provides an easier transition from the ruffle's 8-around structure to the spiral's 10-around.

Finally, the top of the spiral section has a small cap that is crocheted the same way as the endcap in the Endcaps & Ruffles section. By crocheting this second cap section last, you'll have greater leeway when connecting the neckpiece.

If you string the second spiral piece the same way as the first, it will twist in the same direction (both sides twisting to the left, for example). To spiral them in opposite directions, string the beads backward.

Example:
Row 1 = 1B, 1A, 1B, 1A, 1B, 1C, 1E, 1D, 1F, 1C.
Row 2 = String starting with 1C: 1C, 1F, 1D, 1E, 1C, 1B, 1A, 1B, 1A, 1B.

SPIRALS STRINGING PATTERN

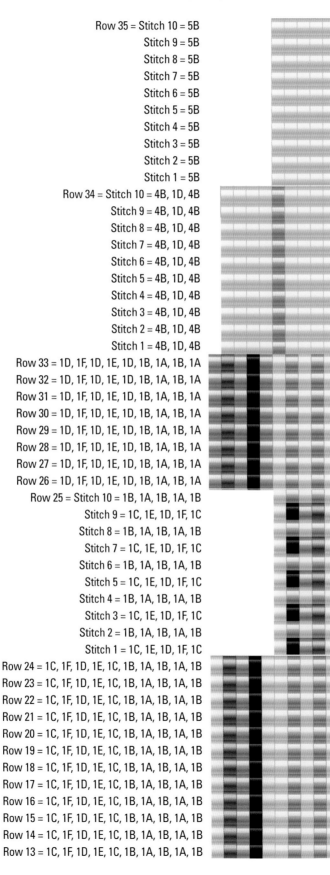

Row 35 = Stitch 10 = 5B
Stitch 9 = 5B
Stitch 8 = 5B
Stitch 7 = 5B
Stitch 6 = 5B
Stitch 5 = 5B
Stitch 4 = 5B
Stitch 3 = 5B
Stitch 2 = 5B
Stitch 1 = 5B
Row 34 = Stitch 10 = 4B, 1D, 4B
Stitch 9 = 4B, 1D, 4B
Stitch 8 = 4B, 1D, 4B
Stitch 7 = 4B, 1D, 4B
Stitch 6 = 4B, 1D, 4B
Stitch 5 = 4B, 1D, 4B
Stitch 4 = 4B, 1D, 4B
Stitch 3 = 4B, 1D, 4B
Stitch 2 = 4B, 1D, 4B
Stitch 1 = 4B, 1D, 4B
Row 33 = 1D, 1F, 1D, 1E, 1D, 1B, 1A, 1B, 1A
Row 32 = 1D, 1F, 1D, 1E, 1D, 1B, 1A, 1B, 1A
Row 31 = 1D, 1F, 1D, 1E, 1D, 1B, 1A, 1B, 1A
Row 30 = 1D, 1F, 1D, 1E, 1D, 1B, 1A, 1B, 1A
Row 29 = 1D, 1F, 1D, 1E, 1D, 1B, 1A, 1B, 1A
Row 28 = 1D, 1F, 1D, 1E, 1D, 1B, 1A, 1B, 1A
Row 27 = 1D, 1F, 1D, 1E, 1D, 1B, 1A, 1B, 1A
Row 26 = 1D, 1F, 1D, 1E, 1D, 1B, 1A, 1B, 1A
Row 25 = Stitch 10 = 1B, 1A, 1B, 1A, 1B
Stitch 9 = 1C, 1E, 1D, 1F, 1C
Stitch 8 = 1B, 1A, 1B, 1A, 1B
Stitch 7 = 1C, 1E, 1D, 1F, 1C
Stitch 6 = 1B, 1A, 1B, 1A, 1B
Stitch 5 = 1C, 1E, 1D, 1F, 1C
Stitch 4 = 1B, 1A, 1B, 1A, 1B
Stitch 3 = 1C, 1E, 1D, 1F, 1C
Stitch 2 = 1B, 1A, 1B, 1A, 1B
Stitch 1 = 1C, 1E, 1D, 1F, 1C
Row 24 = 1C, 1F, 1D, 1E, 1C, 1B, 1A, 1B, 1A, 1B
Row 23 = 1C, 1F, 1D, 1E, 1C, 1B, 1A, 1B, 1A, 1B
Row 22 = 1C, 1F, 1D, 1E, 1C, 1B, 1A, 1B, 1A, 1B
Row 21 = 1C, 1F, 1D, 1E, 1C, 1B, 1A, 1B, 1A, 1B
Row 20 = 1C, 1F, 1D, 1E, 1C, 1B, 1A, 1B, 1A, 1B
Row 19 = 1C, 1F, 1D, 1E, 1C, 1B, 1A, 1B, 1A, 1B
Row 18 = 1C, 1F, 1D, 1E, 1C, 1B, 1A, 1B, 1A, 1B
Row 17 = 1C, 1F, 1D, 1E, 1C, 1B, 1A, 1B, 1A, 1B
Row 16 = 1C, 1F, 1D, 1E, 1C, 1B, 1A, 1B, 1A, 1B
Row 15 = 1C, 1F, 1D, 1E, 1C, 1B, 1A, 1B, 1A, 1B
Row 14 = 1C, 1F, 1D, 1E, 1C, 1B, 1A, 1B, 1A, 1B
Row 13 = 1C, 1F, 1D, 1E, 1C, 1B, 1A, 1B, 1A, 1B

SPIRALS STRINGING PATTERN (CONT'D)

Row 12 = Stitch 10 = 1B, 1A, 1B, 1A, 1B
Stitch 9 = 1C, 1E, 1D, 1F, 1C
Stitch 8 = 1B, 1A, 1B, 1A, 1B
Stitch 7 = 1C, 1E, 1D, 1F, 1C
Stitch 6 = 1B, 1A, 1B, 1A, 1B
Stitch 5 = 1C, 1E, 1D, 1F, 1C
Stitch 4 = 1B, 1A, 1B, 1A, 1B
Stitch 3 = 1C, 1E, 1D, 1F, 1C
Stitch 2 = 1B, 1A, 1B, 1A, 1B
Stitch 1 = 1C, 1E, 1D, 1F, 1C
Row 11 = 1C, 1F, 1D, 1E, 1C, 1B, 1A, 1B, 1A, 1B
Row 10 = 1C, 1F, 1D, 1E, 1C, 1B, 1A, 1B, 1A , 1B
Row 9 = 1C, 1F, 1D, 1E, 1C, 1B, 1A, 1B, 1A , 1B
Row 8 = 1C, 1F, 1D, 1E, 1C, 1B, 1A, 1B, 1A , 1B
Row 7 = 1C, 1F, 1D, 1E, 1C, 1B, 1A, 1B, 1A , 1B
Row 6 = 1C, 1F, 1D, 1E, 1C, 1B, 1A, 1B, 1A , 1B
Row 5 = 1C, 1F, 1D, 1E, 1C, 1B, 1A, 1B, 1A , 1B
Row 4 = 1C, 1F, 1D, 1E, 1C, 1B, 1A, 1B, 1A , 1B
Row 3 = 1C, 1F, 1D, 1E, 1C, 1B, 1A, 1B, 1A , 1B
Row 2 = 1C, 1F, 1D, 1E, 1C, 1B, 1A, 1B, 1A , 1B
Row 1 = 1C, 1F, 1D, 1E, 1C, 1B, 1A, 1B, 1A , 1B

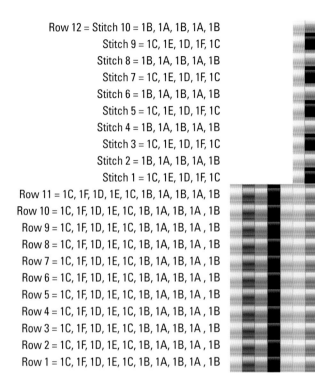

BEAD KEY

A 11º seed beads matte metallic blue

B 11º seed beads metallic bronze

C 8º seed beads matte metallic blue

D 8º seed beads metallic bronze

E 3mm bicones, jet AB

F 3mm bicones, metallic blue AB2x

G 4mm Czech firepolished beads, black AB

NECKPIECE

The "Neckpiece" portion of the project is 160 rows of a repeating pattern; however, if you prefer a shorter or longer section around your neck consider adding or omitting as desired.

The neckpiece is also 10-around. It does not have any crystals or Czech beads, and so creates a much smoother and softer section for around your neck. Also, you don't necessarily want this area competing with the more important areas of the piece in the front.

The example bronze/blue project piece's neckpiece is 12⅞" long.

CONNECTING THE SECTIONS

To connect the sections, use a modified invisible join technique. Sections that connect to either wider or narrower around sections will connect seamlessly as the looser stitches of the ruffles and caps hide the join points. Both neckpiece ends connect to each spiral section's cap area.

Pay close attention to the bead sizes and spiral direction when joining your seams for design consistency. Consider making a second pass on each join area to reinforce the connection point further.

FINISHING OPTIONS

This necklace is finished with the endcaps at the ends and a magnetic closure where the ruffles join. Place the magnetic closure down farther into the Ruffles section, well hidden from view but keeping the Ruffles separated when connected. Feel free to finish with a beautiful focal bead and/or separately sewn on fringes after the cap beads—the options are yours to choose!

If you plan to wear this necklace frequently, reinforce the spiral section of crystals.

NECKPIECE STRINGING PATTERN

Rows 1-160 = 1A, 1B, 1A, 1B, 1A, 2B, 2A, 1D

BEAD KEY

A 11º seed beads matte metallic blue

B 11º seed beads metallic bronze

C 8º seed beads matte metallic blue

D 8º seed beads metallic bronze

Contributors

Rifka Boswell
Rifka Boswell contributed designs and tested many patterns. Rifka has been involved in the beading world since the early '90s. She lives and works in Sahuarita, Ariz.

Linda Lehman
Linda Lehman loves wearing two hats in the world of bead crochet: designer and teacher. Linda is the author of the book *Bead Crochet Jewelry*, and her work has been published in *Bead&Button* magazine. She teaches bead crochet at national bead conventions, beading guilds, and beading stores. Look for her work at etsy.com/shop/wearableartemporium.

Leila Martin
Leila is the owner of Bella Beads in Marquette, Mich. (shopbellabeads.com). She loves many forms of jewelry making, including metal clay, metalsmithing, wireworking, and freeform seed bead work, but she favors the simplicity of bead crochet because it's easy to pick up in a moment when a beading craving comes on.

Yoshie Marubashi
Originally from Japan, Yoshie is a well-known bead crochet designer who now lives in Forest Hills, N.Y. Her beadwork has won awards in *Bead&Button* magazine's Bead Dreams contest, and her work has been published in *500 Beaded Objects*.

Acknowledgments

This book would not be possible without the support and encouragement of my family: my husband, Bob, and my children, Allie, Sam, and Chris. Thank you for your patience and for surrendering the kitchen and dining room tables (and various other parts of the house) to beading projects and kits.

Beading friends have always been so supportive, and I'd like to especially thank Rifka Boswell, who helped make samples, tested patterns tirelessly, and is a contributor to this book. Thanks to the "Stitchy Witches" group for your continued friendship and encouragement: Mel, Sue, and Debbie (thanks for checking patterns!), as well as Beth, Carol, and Karol. A big thank you to Sue Wade for the opportunity to teach at her shop. Lydia Borin, Adele Rogers Recklies, and Karen Flowers answered technical questions and gave guidance during this process, and Julia Gerlach was our expert technical editor. I thank you all as well.

Contributors have been integral to the wealth of designs in this book. In addition to Rifka, huge thank yous go to Yoshie Marubashi, Leila Martin, and Linda Lehman.

Despite time and careful attention reviewing directions, checking patterns, and revising illustrations, I am sure that my readers will note corrections that are needed. I appreciate your input. Please send any information and suggestions to me via my website, candicesexton.com. Check my site for supplementary pattern information.

I'd like to thank Mary Wohlgemuth for starting this odyssey with me as well as the Kalmbach Books team for crafting a beautiful book: Dianne Wheeler, Lisa Bergman, Bill Zuback, Jim Forbes, Julia Gerlach, and Karin Van Voorhees.

About the author

Candice Sexton discovered bead crochet in 2001 when traveling with beadwork on airplanes became a challenge. She loves the relaxing, meditative, and creative qualities of bead crochet, and she also enjoys beadweaving and wireworking. Candice delights in devising new and unusual ways to work with materials and techniques, such as creating the ruffles technique and using wire as a cord for sewing beads.

Candice's work has been published in both *Bead&Button* and *Perlen Poesie* magazines. She teaches locally in her home state of Indiana and nationally at the *Bead&Button Show* and *Bead Fest.*

Candice has a bachelor's degree in construction and a master's degree in media communication. She works as an advertising and marketing professional. Her varied background includes working as an engineer, publishing a women's magazine, and working in catalog design and development. Visit her website at candicesexton.com and her etsy store at etsy.com/shop/candicesexton.

Your complete guide
to creating kumihimo jewelry!

Kumihimo
BASICS & BEYOND
24 braided and beaded jewelry projects on the kumihimo disk

Rebecca Ann Combs

67020
$21.99

"Kumihimo Basics & Beyond will be my go-to source for all things kumihimo! Rebecca addresses tension, thread size, patterns, and so much more. You'll even find 'math' charts that take the guesswork out of kumihimo, with and without beads. It's the perfect recipe for success!"

— Jane Danley Cruz,
Associate Editor,
Bead&Button magazine

Create all-cord braids and beaded braids in no time with Rebecca Combs' book, *Kumihimo Basics & Beyond*.

Short, easy-to-grasp demonstrations of key techniques allow you to learn and practice as you go. Rebecca demystifies "kumihimo math" by teaching you how to calculate the amount of fiber and number of beads you'll need for your own future projects.

Buy now from your favorite bead or craft shop!
Or at www.KalmbachStore.com or call 1-800-533-6644

Monday – Friday, 8:30 a.m. – 4:30 p.m. CT. Outside the United States and Canada call 262-796-8776, ext. 661.

 www.facebook.com/KalmbachJewelryBooks   www.pinterest.com/kalmbachjewelry

P22314

2XBB